13-0

THE
CHAMPIONSHIP
SEASON

Cover Design: Ray Brown
Designer: Lori Leath-Smith

Printed by Ebsco Media, Birmingham, Alabama

ISBN 0-9635413-0-7

INDEX

The eye of the Tide; The look of a champion.

The
National
Championship

``We're the national champion and, brother, that's big. That's what you work for all year. That's what our players worked for since spring training. You know, it's great to have goals, but it's a whole lot better when you reach them."

—Alabama coach Gene Stallings

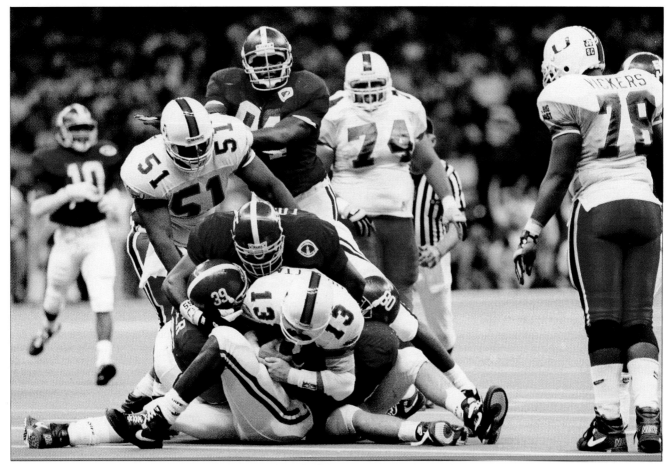

Alabama's storied defense vs. Miami's storied quarterback. The winner took all.

The National Championship

by Charles Hollis

It seems like a fairytale to Alabama coach Gene Stallings. Something out of the movies. Something out of somebody's imagination.

Real life can't be like this. Not this good.

``I don't have the vocabulary for the right words to describe everything our football team has accomplished this year,'' said Stallings, who was hired in January of 1990 to replace Bill Curry and ressurect the Alabama championship tradition. ``When you look at all the things we've accomplished this year, it's sort of hard to believe.

``This is one of those teams and one of those sea-

sons you'll remember the rest of your life. But it's sort of hard to believe, isn't it?''

In the school's 100th year of football, the Crimson Tide won it all. Every game. Everything.

To go 13-0, to win the Southeastern Conference West Division, to win the inaugural SEC Championship Game in Birmingham, to beat 8 1/2-point favorite Miami 34-13 in the Sugar Bowl and win the college football national championship, is still hard for Stallings to comprehend.

`I'm going to enjoy talking about this team and this season in the off-season, I can assure you,'' he said.

And that winning streak—23 in a row, the longest

in the nation after snapping Miami's 29-game string—makes Stallings shake his head in amazement, too.

``In this day and time and with so many teams close to each other in ability, that's hard to do. That's a lot of games we've won. And you know, we're going to be a pretty good team next year.''

The 13 wins, the SEC and national titles, the coach of the year honors, all of that seemed so far away to Stallings back in August.

Alabama was hurting at quarterback, placekicker, punter and there was little or no depth at linebacker and in the defensive backfield.

Alabama had a quarterback, third-year sophomore Jay Barker of Trussville, but Barker lacked quarterback experience. ``You don't become a successful quarterback overnight,'' said Stallings. ``In Jay's case, he was a quarterback his senior year in high school, in an option offense, and that was the extent of his quarterback experience before he came to Alabama.''

Alabama had a field goal kicker, true freshman Michael Proctor of Pelham, who had been highly recruited. But Proctor had never kicked against Tennessee and Auburn.

Alabama had what Stallings felt was a prospect for punter, third-year sophomore Bryne Diehl of Oakman, but Diehl had a tendency to be erratic.

``We were going to have a good defense and a good running game, but you've also got to have a good kicking game,'' Stallings said. ``If you're not sound in the kicking game, it'll come back to haunt you.''

Some how, some way, the pieces came together.

Barker became the quarterback who always seemed to do enough of the right things to help the offense win.

Proctor became a record-breaking kicker, setting

school records for most points in a season (94) and field goals in a game (4) by a freshman.

And Diehl, he seemed to kick better as the season progressed. He had one nightmare game, against Florida in the SEC title game when three consecutive punts traveled 16, 19 and 25 yards.

Still, Alabama beat the Gators 28-21, and in its usual fashion with the defense saving the day. This time it was junior cornerback Antonio Langham, the MVP of the game, intercepting a Shane Matthews pass with three minutes to go and returning it 27 yards for the winning score.

"I've said it a gillion times, but you play 50 or 60 plays a game for the privilege of making three or four or five plays that will make the difference,'' Stallings said. ``Brother, that was a big play Antonio made against Florida.

``If we don't beat Florida and win the championship game, we don't play Miami for the national championship. But it seems like it's been like that all year. It seems like every game was a big one.

``We started off the year with Vanderbilt and that was a big game for us because it was our first division game.

"You've got to win your division before you can play for the conference championship. The Arkansas game was big because it was our first conference road game and the first SEC game between the two schools.

``When we played Tennessee in Knoxville, that was big. Then it seemed like every week after that

THE TOP 25

The Top Twenty Five teams in the Associated Press 1992 final football poll, with first-place votes in parentheses, records, total points based on 25 points for a first-place vote through one point for a 25th-place vote, and previous ranking:

	Record	Pts.	Pvs.
1. **Alabama** (62)	13-0-0	1,550	2
2. **Florida St.**	11-1-0	1,470	3
3. **Miami**	11-1-0	1,410	1
4. **Notre Dame**	10-1-1	1,375	5
5. **Michigan**	9-0-3	1,266	7
6. **Syracuse**	10-2-0	1,209	6
7. **Texas A&M**	12-1-0	1,167	4
8. **Georgia**	10-2-0	1,159	8
9. **Stanford**	10-3-0	1,058	13
10. **Florida**	9-4-0	931	14
11. **Washington**	9-3-0	892	9
12. **Tennessee**	9-3-0	819	17
13. **Colorado**	9-2-1	818	10
14. **Nebraska**	9-3-0	771	11
15. **Wash. St.**	9-3-0	618	18
16. **Mississippi**	9-3-0	583	20
17. **N. Car. St.**	9-3-1	582	12
18. **Ohio St.**	8-3-1	493	15
19. **N. Carolina**	9-3-0	491	19
20. **Hawaii**	11-2-0	354	—
21. **Boston Coll.**	8-3-1	314	16
22. **Kansas**	8-4-0	183	—
23. **Mississippi St.**	7-5-0	167	24
24. **Fresno St.**	9-4-0	124	—
25. **Wake Forest**	8-4-0	107	—

Sherman Williams drives into the end zone for a touchdown against the Hurricanes

every game we played was big. Ole Miss, LSU, Mississippi State, Auburn.

``After we beat Auburn we're 11-0 but we hadn't won anything.

"We put everything we had into the Auburn game and now we have to turn around and play Florida for the championship. Brother, that's hard to do.

``I had the feeling after Florida played Florida State (and lost 45-24), it wasn't the emotional game for Florida the Auburn game was for us. The Florida game was not one of our better games. But it was a win, and got us to the Sugar Bowl.''

There also were big decisions along the way, perhaps none bigger or more controversial than Stallings' decision to let star wide receiver/kick returner David Palmer return to action. Palmer sat out the Sept. 5 opener against Vanderbilt as punishment for a drunken driving arrest over the summer.

Just when it looked like Palmer had gotten out of Stallings' doghouse, he got back in it. He was arrested

on a second DUI offense less than 10 hours after the Vandy game, creating even more headlines and negative publicity for himself, Stallings and the university.

After consulting with the administration, numerous counselors, psychologists and legal experts, Stallings decided to bring his star player back in the fourth game of the year, against Lousiana Tech.

``Coach Stallings made a decision to help a player

> **"I love playing in the 'Dome. Do the Saints need a running back?"**
> *—Alabama runner Derrick Lassic*

help himself," said co-captain Prince Wimbley. ``He could have kicked David off the team, but that wouldn't have helped David. David needed the team more than we needed him. And Coach Stallings knew

Donnie Finkley, Derrick Lassic and Prince Wimbley in their championship poses

(23-34-1). I don't know the right words to explain how much I appreciate them for taking a chance on me. I've told them that, too."

"Brother, am I a lucky man. Only in America can

> **``That play George Teague made when he took the ball away may be the finest by play an Alabama player ever made.''**
> —*Alabama defensive assistant coach Bill Oliver*

you be fired twice and be Coach of the Year."

A team that would not be denied

by Charles Hollis

NEW ORLEANS—There was something different in the Alabama dressing room before its biggest game of the year. Something quarterback Jay Barker couldn't put his finger on. Something he noticed right away.

``It was so quiet you could hear a pin drop," said Barker.

``It was never like that before. No one was talking. Nobody was saying anything. It's never been that quiet this year before a game."

Barker said players were staring at the floor, looking at the walls. Just staring into space. They were in their own world.

``All we could picture in our mind was beating

Miami," said senior running back Derrick Lassic. ``We were focused on Miami and what we had to do to win it. Maybe we were obsessed. We wanted this game more than Miami. We wanted respect and you get respect by beating great teams like Miami.

``Yeah, it was real quiet before the game. But no one had to say anything. We knew what we had to do. We knew we had to go out and play the game of our life. I think we came as close as we could, if we didn't do it."

Alabama, ranked No. 2 in the nation, upset Miami, ranked No. 1 in the nation, with a resounding 34-13 victory New Year's night in the USF&G Sugar Bowl. ``They say good things come to those who wait," said Lassic, who has been waiting five years to start in the backfield and to lead the team in rushing. He ran for 135 yards and finished with 1,040 yards and 12 touchdowns this year.

But much more important than yards and touchdowns and most valuable player honors in the Sugar

Bowl, according to Lassic, the Tide will get national championship rings. ``Real big rings," he said, grinning. ``The kind you can see a mile away. The kind Miami players were flashing in our faces all week. ``This was our quest, our goal, our destiny. We were

> ``I told Torretta I would see him all night, and he knew it. The key to the game was to flush out Torretta and keep him from getting into his rhythm."
>
> —*Alabama defensive end Eric Curry*

going to win this game, no matter what it took," added Lassic.

``You could see it in everybody's face in the dressing room how much they wanted to win this game.

Torretta sorts out confusion in the early going, but never solved the problem

George Teague, Roosevelt Patterson and Alvin Hope celebrate victory over Miami

I've never felt so much intensity.

``Nobody said a word before the game. But nobody had to say a word. You could see the intensity when we left the hotel to come to the 'Dome. You could feel the emotion on this team. You could sense something was about to happen.

``The Miami players did a lot of talking this week, but by the second quarter (with Alabama holding a 10-3 lead) you didn't hear too much from them. ``By the end of the third quarter (and a 27-6 Alabama lead) we were doing the talking instead of Miami. It was nice to shut them up. They did so much talking before the game, how they were going to do this to us or that to us. They talked their trash. But we shut them up early. ``I don't think they ever imagined Alabama was going to dominate the game like we did—just

blow them out. We handled them pretty good. I think they have a greater respect for Alabama now than they did a few days ago.''

The Tide offense came into the game looking for

> ``I wanted so badly for Gino to look my way when I popped open, but I knew he was being forced out of the pocket.''
>
> —*Miami flanker Kevin Williams*

respect. After a season of getting kicked around and being the butt of jokes, center Tobie Sheils said the offense wanted respect.

``Everybody said the Miami defense would own us,'' said Sheils. ``We owned them. I think we surprised ourselves.

We were controlling the game so well with our running game, we were knocking Miami off the line, that some of our guys would come back to the huddle and say, `We're killing them. Let's keep running right at them.''

Led by Lassic's 135 yards on 28 carries, the offense produced 285 yards, with 267 on the ground. No opponent had manhandled the Miami defense like that.

Even though the Hurricanes had more first down (16 to 15) and more yards (326 to 285) than Alabama,

the Tide kept the ball 36 minutes to Miami's 24 minutes and had two turnovers to three for Miami.

Alabama's two turnovers were in the first half, both were interceptions by Barker.

``If you had told me before the game I was going to throw two interceptions in the first half, I would have said we're going to lose the game,'' said Barker. ``And if you'd said we were only going to pass for 18 yards (on 4-of-13 passing), I would have thought for sure it was going to be a long game for us.''

But Barker expected Miami, one of the fastest defenses in the country, to be impenetrable. ``But they were not as good as Louisiana Tech or Auburn. I'm sorry, but I still feel Louisiana Tech and Auburn were better. ``I don't mean any disrespect, but we handled

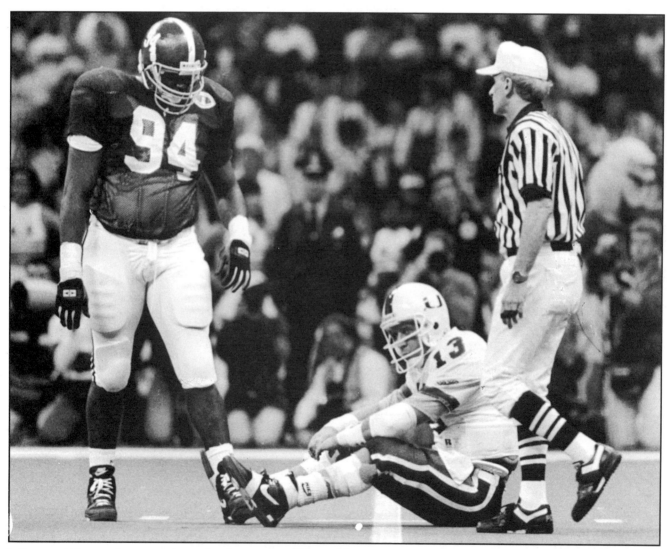

A disgusted Torretta is towered over by the source of his problems

Stallings confers on sideline during Miami game

``I could say some things, but I won't. But all I read and hear was how our offense was going to have a hard time with their defense.

``I was asked earlier in the week if we could run on Miami, and I felt we could. But I don't think anyone believed me.

I don't think anyone really respected our offense. But we put in some things, especially the traps, that allowed us to get our running game established early in the game.

``We had an excellent plan. Coach Stallings did an excellent job getting our team ready to play. And now we've won the national championship."

Moore spent 22 years at Alabama. He was offensive coordinator in 1979 on the Alabama team that defeated Penn State for the national championship, the school's last.

Miami a lot better than we handled Louisiana Tech and Auburn."

A big part of Alabama's success were the trap plays put in for Miami. Instead of power blocking or blocking the defensive front left or right, assistant head coach Mal Moore said the plan called for trapping the Hurricane front and exploiting their aggressiveness.

``It's like a dream-type ending for this team. To go 13-0 and win the first SEC title game. Now we beat the No. 1 team in the nation in a game we're not supposed to win.

``Maybe now we can get some respect."

Time for Miami to eat some words

by Kevin Scarbinsky

NEW ORLEANS—When the Alabama football players raced onto the field Friday night in the Louisiana Superdome before the 59th annual Sugar Bowl, the Miami football players turned their backs.

When the Alabama football captains advanced to midfield before the game for the coin toss, the Miami captains did not shake their hands.

These are traditions with the Hurricanes, same as winning national championships is a tradition. Miami was poised to win its second straight national championship Friday night, its fourth in six years, its fifth in 10 years, the last two feats unprecedented in college football history.

Instead, Miami lost the game and its chance to make history. The team that wouldn't shake hands could only shake its head and let the past ease the crushing blow of the present.

``After the game, I couldn't decide whether to cry,'' Miami senior cornerback Ryan McNeil said. ``Then I thought, `What have I got to cry about? I've had a great career. This game doesn't ruin that.' ''

The game did ruin Miami's ability to back up its boastful pregame talk. Wideout Lamar Thomas said Alabama cornerbacks George Teague and Antonio

Not every play went Alabama's way. This pass was picked off by Miami.

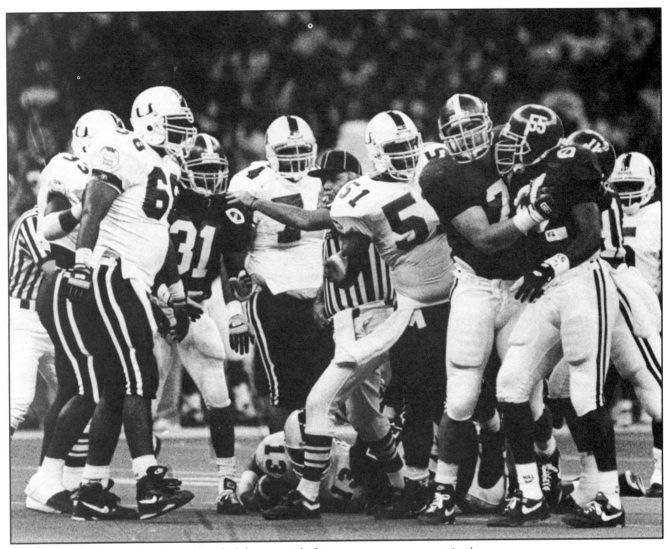

Lippy Miami players and unintimidated Alabama made for some tense moments in the game

Langham were overrated because they played zone most of the time rather than man-to-man defense. Thomas was caught from behind twice and stripped of the ball twice, resulting in turnovers: Once by cornerback Tommy Johnson after a 13-yard gain to the Alabama 23, once by Teague after an 82-yard gain to the Alabama 7.

Thomas turned contrite after the game.
``Give Alabama credit,'' he said. ``They deserve it. Their offense dominated. Their defense dominated. Give them all the credit.''

Several Miami defensive players said before the game that no one-dimensional offense such as Alabama's could move the ball against them. The Crimson Tide was one-dimensional Friday night, throwing for just 18 yards. But Alabama ran for 267 yards and con-trolled the ball for 36 minutes.

``I can see now,'' Miami linebacker Micheal Barrow said, ``why they don't need to pass.''
Miami quarterback Gino Torretta did not say anything derogatory toward Alabama before the game, but his

> ``It doesn't make any difference if we're number 2, number 3 or number 4.''
>
> —*Miami coach Dennis Erickson*

play Friday night said something derogatory about him. He hit 24 passes but missed 32. He did not throw a touchdown pass but did throw three interceptions.

Two of those interceptions came on Miami's first two plays of the second half. Alabama used the first one to

> **``Once we started playing Miami-style defense, it was too late.''**
> —*Miami linebacker Micheal Barrow*

set up a touchdown and returned the second one for a touchdown to turn a 13-6 halftime lead into a 27-6 laugher.

``The whole game was a blur,'' Torretta said. ``I don't even remember what happened in the second half.'' In both halves, the Alabama secondary confused Torretta with a kaleidoscope of looks, which he had little time to straighten out because the Alabama pass rush did not allow him much time. Alabama ignored Miami's running game—weak all year, it gained 48 worthless yards Friday—and teed off on Torretta.

Sugar Bowl MVP Derrick Lassic gains yardage against the highly touted Miami defense

Stallings never felt his team an underdog

by Charles Hollis

NEW ORLEANS—Away from the crowd, away from reporters asking his players how they pulled off one of the biggest upsets of the college football season, Alabama coach Gene Stallings was at peace with the world.

His wife, Ruth Ann, and his youngest daughter, Martha Kate, were outside the dressing room when he returned from his postgame press conference, just before midnight Friday. They showered Stallings with kisses and hugs and told him how proud they were that No. 2 Alabama defeated No. 1 Miami.

``Gene, it'll take you an hour to hug everybody in your family, as many kids as you've got,'' said offensive line coach Jim Fuller, interrupting the mushy stuff.

``This is so wonderful, so thrilling for everyone in our family,'' said Ruth Ann Stallings. ``This has to be one of the happiest and proudest moments for everybody in our family.

``I'm so happy for Gene and the football team. They've worked so hard and been through so much this year.''

Stallings walked into a private office in the team dressing room and was met by his son, Johnny, who has Down's syndrome.

Both father

Defensive back George Teague knocks away pass from Miami receiver Kevin Williams

and son shared a moment together. ``Great job, Pop,'' said Johnny. ``You did OK, Pop.'' Stallings looked at Johnny and placed a national championship cap on his head. ``We're national champions, partner,'' Stallings said. ``The national champion, son. That's big.''

What a nice way to ring in the 101st year of Alabama football and write the final chapter to Stallings' third year at Alabama, a year that included an SEC title, a 13-0 record, numerous coach of the year honors and the national championship.

The 34 points the Tide scored were the most against Miami since Tennessee's 35-7 upset win in the 1987 Sugar Bowl.

``I know our team and staff accomplished something truly big, but it hasn't really hit me yet,'' Stallings

Lassic runs away from Miami defenders in a 100-yard plus effort

said in the dressing room. ``I know there were a lot of people out there who felt we didn't have a chance; felt we were a big underdog. But it didn't surprise me we won the game.

``If you'll go back and check, you'll see I never said we were the underdog. First of all, I didn't believe we were the underdog. I felt we had a good football team and had a good chance to win the game.

``Miami's a good football team. I thought they were well-prepared. But deep down, I didn't think they were better than we were. I felt we were a pretty good defensive team. I felt we could do some things to keep them off-balance. Even though you don't win with schemes, I thought we had a good scheme.

``I don't consider this an upset.''

Tight end Steve Busky is helped from the field after colliding with another player when Alabama tried to keep a punt from going into the end zone.

Secondary coach Bill Oliver, the architect of Alabama's nationally ranked defense, devised a scheme that played mind games with quarterback Gino Torretta.

Even though Torretta was a fifth-year senior and the Heisman Trophy winner, Oliver felt he could trick Torretta into thinking Alabama was in man coverage when it really was in zone, and vice versa.

Oliver felt Torretta's eyes would get as big as his postseason honors if he saw Alabama defensive backs on the line of scrimmage and staring into the faces of Miami receivers Lamar Thomas, Horace Copeland and Kevin Williams.

``We took some chances, but you've got to take some chances against the kind of talent Miami puts on the field,'' said Oliver. ``I saw our kids making as many big plays in a game as I've ever seen.''

The defense

was so effective with its strategy that Miami had two first downs and 133 yards the first half. As for Torretta, considered the best quarterback in the country because of his Heisman honor, he was thoroughly confused.

Torretta hit 12-of-25 passes for 127 yards and was intercepted once in the first half. Miami's only points came on two Dane Prewitt field goals, from 49 and 42 yards out. The 49-yarder was the longest of the Hewitt-Trussville High grad's career.

Torretta had a miserable performance, completing 24-of-56 passes for 278 yards and three interceptions. Sam Shade, Tommy Johnson and George Teague all had pick-offs.

``Everybody was talking about Torretta and their receivers,'' said Shade. ``The Miami players did a lot of talking about how we hadn't faced anybody like them. Somewhere in the third quarter they stopped telling us how good they were and how they were going to beat us.''

A grim Dennis Erickson accepts his fate following the game

As one-dimensional as the Tide was with its running game, the Hurricanes were just as one-dimensional. Their Achilles heel, the run, produced only 48 yards in the game.

``We knew their defense was good, but they were probably a little better than we expected,'' said wide receiver Kevin Williams. ``I think their speed surprised us. They could match us with speed, and nobody has done that before.''

Miami's only touchdown did not come from the offense. It came from the special teams, a 78-yard punt return in the fourth quarter by Kevin Williams.

``I said before the game that we hadn't played our best game of the year; that it was still out there,'' said Stallings. ``I think we finally put everything together—offense, defense, special teams—to play our best game.

``I know we gave up the long punt return, but we also covered kicks as well as we have all year. I couldn't begin to name all the players who made big plays for us. I know I saw (defensive back) Tommy Johnson knock down a touchdown pass in the end zone on fourth down. I know I saw (defensive back) George Teague run down (Lamar) Thomas after a long pass and strip him of the ball. He caught him from behind and took the ball away from him. That was a big-league play, the kind you see in the National Football League.

ESPN made Teague's pick-pocket play the play of

Miami players console each other as it becomes apparent their winning streak is about to end

the day on its late-night telecast.

``I know (running back) Derrick Lassic played as well as I've ever seen him play,'' Stallings continued. ``I mean, he ran hard. I know our offensive line knocked people off the line. I know (kick returner/receiver) David Palmer made some key plays.''

Stallings noticed early in the week there was a high level of intensity, more so than usual. On Sunday, the scout-team offense had two players who sustained injuries, courtesy of the nation's top defense. And

there was a fight that broke out on Monday.

``When players are coming in two and three hours before their 11 p.m. curfew, when not a single player out of 145 football players are late, that says something,'' said Stallings.

``This team was ready to play when we got to New Orleans last Saturday,'' added Stallings. ``I didn't have to give a big pep talk. I just had to make sure they didn't play the game on Wednesday or Thursday.''

Tucson writer Corky Simpson knew all along. Here's his story:

Corky Simpson, 54, sports columnist for the Tucson (Ariz.)Citizen, voted Alabama No. 1 for all 17 weeks of The Associated Press college football poll, including the preseason. The team received no other No. 1 votes.

by Corky Simpson
The Tucson Citizen

TUCSON, Ariz.—Vindication isn't mine, it's Alabama's.

As the only voter in The Associated Press Top 25 poll who picked the Crimson Tide No. 1 every week, I took my share of flak from around the country, but that's part of the game.

I stuck with the kids from Alabama because they gave me no choice. How do you bail out on a team that refused to lose?

Genius? Nah, I'm the same guy who picked the New England Patriots to beat the Chicago Bears a few years ago in the Super Bowl.

The last winner I picked was a horse named Chateaugay in the Kentucky Derby, years before any of the Alabama players were born. But I knew this Alabama team was special because I did something others apparently failed to do: homework.

Believe it or not, I cast my first ballot for the Crimson Tide last February.

In a preseason poll conducted by the Football Writer's Association of America at the NCAA College Football Forum in Kansas City, I picked the Tide to be No. 1 in the nation.

I took the time to talk to Alabama coach Gene Stallings; to a good friend, Bill Lumpkin, a sports editor in Birmingham, and to Larry White of the Alabama sports information office. I looked at the talent on this Alabama team and became convinced the Tide would field one of the greatest defensive units in college football. Games are won on defense, and that is more than a cliché in football.

Over the summer, The Associated Press gave me the opportunity to cast the Arizona ballot in its week-

Jay Barker and Tommy Johnson celebrate victory

ly poll, and I was pleased to take part.

But at one point during the season I wondered if I might not lose my voting privilege. I worried that I might be embarrassing the AP.

Irate telephone calls and nasty letters to my newspaper, mostly from Miami fans, came pouring in after Mark Edwards of *The Decatur Daily* in Alabama revealed my identity.

One man in Miami threatened to fax me his rear end. A woman in Florida wrote that I was ``morally irresponsible and inherently evil'' for voting for Alabama.

The Los Angeles Times raised the question as to what kind of moonshine I had been drinking. I had the chance to talk to Pete Rose, too, on his talk show in Florida. He gave mc a good ribbing, said that Miami was by far the better team, and surprised me with a keen understanding of college football.

Every vote I cast in the AP poll, from the preseason through the final ballot after the bowl games, was based on my honest opinion. It was not to attract attention.

The chance of this ever happening again, or having happened in the first place, must be a zillion to one. I was right all along, it turns out, but not, I'm sorry to say, because I am brilliant—only because I did my homework.

It was an interesting adventure. Most of it was in fun and I never once doubted my vote. Even when Washington and Miami were riding high, and Alabama was just slipping by, something told me fate was with the Crimson Tide.

After all, this is Alabama's centennial year of football.

So maybe the ghost of Bear Bryant was somewhere on the sidelines next to his former player, coach Gene Stallings.

A Miami defender slaps at one of Alabama's few pass attempts

Torretta a marked man

by Kevin Scarbinsky

The best thing a college football player can do is win the Heisman Trophy, which marks him as the best player in the country. The worst thing a college football player can do is win the Heisman Trophy, which marks him for almost certain defeat come bowl time.

Miami quarterback Gino Torretta won the Heisman Trophy three weeks ago, but Friday night he played what he called the worst game of his career in the 34-13 loss to Alabama in the Sugar Bowl. With the national championship on the line, Torretta completed 24-of-56 passes for 278

John Copeland and Eric Curry celebrate a defensive play as Miami player remains down

yards, but he did not direct his offense to a touchdown and he did throw three interceptions, each of which led to an Alabama touchdown.

With that dismal performance, Torretta joined the growing list of Heisman winners and bowl losers. Only two Heisman winners since 1980 have won their bowl games: 1984 winner Doug Flutie and Boston College beat Houston in the Cotton Bowl, and 1988 winner Barry Sanders and Oklahoma State beat Wyoming in the Holiday Bowl.

The previous Heisman winners/bowl losers: **1980**—George Rogers and South Carolina lose to Pitt in the Gator Bowl; **1981**—Marcus Allen and USC lose

> ``I don't worry about my statistics. My job is to lead. If we win, I'm happy.''
>
> —*Alabama quarterback Jay Barker*

to Penn State in the Fiesta; **1982**—Herschel Walker and Georgia lose to Penn State in the Sugar; **1983**—Mike Rozier and Nebraska lose to Miami in the Orange; **1985**—Bo Jackson and Auburn lose to Texas A&M in the Cotton; **1986**—Vinny Testaverde and Miami lose to Penn State in the Fiesta; **1987**—Tim Brown and Notre Dame lose to Texas A&M in the Cotton; **1990**—Ty Detmer and BYU lose to Texas A&M in the Holiday; and **1991**—Desmond Howard and Michigan lose to Washington in the Rose. Houston quarterback Andre Ware, the **1989** Heisman winner, did not play in a bowl game because the Cougars were on NCAA probation.

Rogers glad to be spectator

by Charles Hollis

Alabama sophomore linebacker Michael Rogers wanted to play in the worst way against top-ranked Miami. And he knows if it hadn't been for a car accident he was in on Christmas Eve morning he would have have been in the starting lineup.

``But I'm thankful I was able to go to the game and I'm alive. It's scary to think about what could have happened to me.''

Rogers, a starting inside linebacker, was released from Montgomery's Baptist Hospital Wednesday. He traveled with his older brother, Lamar, a former Auburn defensive lineman, to the game Thursday just in time to be at practice.

> ``If we go out and work hard, I think we can repeat.''
> —*Alabama receiver David Palmer*

The former Luverne High School star watched from the sideline as his teammates upset Miami 34-13.

``There's no way I was going to miss this game in person when I got out of the hospital,'' Rogers said. Rogers was a backseat passenger in a one-car accident near Greenville. The accident killed one passenger and injured two others besides him. Rogers sustained a concussion and bruises and spent four days in intensive care.

Lassic's good luck charm

Derrick Lassic could scarcely pronounce his name and definitely could not spell it, but somewhere in the Superdome crowd Friday night stood a man who brings him luck.

Lassic spoke of one of his high school assistant

Offensive line surges such as this one made Alabama's ground game work all night

coaches from Haverstraw, N.Y., who found his way to New Orleans for the Sugar Bowl.

``He's never seen me lose,'' Lassic said, ``and he's never seen me rush for less than 100 yards. I'm glad he was here. He's my good-luck charm.''

So what's his name? ``Dee Gerolimo? (Geronimo?) Don't even ask me how to spell it.''

Whatever the coach's name, he brought Lassic luck. The senior rushed for 135 yards, scored two touchdowns and won the Miller-Digby Award as most valuable player.

SEC flexes its muscle

by Kevin Scarbinsky

Who was that man walking around the Superdome with a smile on his face Friday night? That was SEC commissioner Roy Kramer.

For years, Kramer's conference has proclaimed itself the best football conference in America. For years, that claim has been toothless come bowl time.

But in the span of little more than 24 hours, the SEC staked an indisputable claim to the top of the

Quarterback Torretta turns defender and grabs Shade's facemask to keep an interception from becoming a touchdown

Georgia did it. The last time the SEC as a league went unbeaten in bowl games was 1960, when the league went 2-0-1.

The league's work was not done after Alabama's win. But North Carolina squeaked by Mississippi State 21-17 in the Peach Bowl Saturday night, for the SEC's only defeat.

Come on refs!

by Kevin Scarbnisky

The penalty? Unsportsmanlike conduct.

The guilty party? Alabama tailback Derrick Lassic.

The explanation? Excessive celebration.

Lassic had just spun his way around left end for 10 yards and a first down at the Miami 1-yard line. A facemask penalty along the way would inch the ball closer to the game's first touchdown.

football world. Five SEC teams played bowl games Thursday and Friday and five of them won. The closest margin of victory was one touchdown.

On Thursday, Florida beat North Carolina State 27-10 in the Gator Bowl and Ole Miss beat Air Force 13-0 in the Liberty Bowl. On Friday, Tennessee beat Boston College 38-23 in the Hall of Fame Bowl and Georgia beat Ohio State 21-14 in the Citrus Bowl.

And in the matter of the SEC's host game, the Sugar Bowl, conference champion and No. 2-ranked Alabama beat No. 1 Miami to claim the national championship. The last time an SEC team finished unbeaten and won the national title was in 1980, when

Except that as Lassic picked himself up, he spun the ball on the ground like a top ``because I was excited. It was a pretty good play.''

As celebrations go, this one was tame—except to the official standing at the goal line. He dropped his flag and whistled Lassic for unsportsmanlike conduct, a 15-yard penalty that took Alabama from first-and-goal at the 1-yard line to first-and-goal at the 16. ``I don't think the official should have made that call in a game of this magnitude,'' Lassic said. ``We didn't just have to beat Miami out there.''

Alabama coach Gene Stallings howled at the call,

Gene Stallings takes issue with a call on the field

and his team had to settle for a field goal—instead of an almost certain touchdown—and a 6-3 lead in the second quarter.

``I didn't see what happened,'' Stallings said. ``I thought the call was pretty severe myself.''

Teague into the end zone, finally

by Kevin Scarbnisky

George Teague had played 45 games for Alabama at cornerback and safety, made 149 tackles, broke up

25 passes, intercepted 14 passes and returned them for 115 yards. Only three people in Alabama history—Jeremiah Castille, John Mangum and Harry Gilmer, all with 16—have intercepted more career passes for the Crimson Tide.

But never in his honored career had Teague returned an interception for a touchdown until the final

> ``They knew we were going to throw on every down. When you do that and you can't stop their pass rush, you can't expect to win.''
>
> —*Miami quarterback Gino Torretta*

game of his Alabama career.

After Alabama cornerback Tommy Johnson intercepted Miami quarterback Gino Torretta's first pass of the second half and returned it 23 yards to set up a touchdown for a 20-6 lead, Teague intercepted Torretta's second pass of the second half and returned it 31 yards all the way to the end zone for a 27-6 lead.
``I've never been in the end zone with a football before,'' Teague said. ``I hate it had to come in my last year in my last game.''

It was his last game for Alabama, but not his last college game. Teague departed New Orleans at 8 o'clock Saturday morning on his way to the Japan Bowl all-star game for college seniors along with teammates Eric Curry and John Copeland. When he returns, Teague will play in the Senior Bowl all-star game in Mobile with teammates Copeland, Curry, Martin Houston, Derrick Lassic, Antonio London, Derrick Oden and Prince Wimbley.

Michael Proctor ended the season as he began it, successfully knocking field goals for the Tide

Teague's running steals a moment to remember

by Kevin Scarbinsky

NEW ORLEANS—Moments. You remember Alabama 34, Miami 13, in moments.

One moment. Alabama crowds eight men at the line of scrimmage in a stare-down with 76,789 witnesses. Miami quarterback Gino Torretta, another fraud in Heisman clothing, blinks and calls time. It's the first quarter. It's the first sign.

``You could see it in his eyes when he came to the line,'' Alabama destroyer John Copeland said. ``He wasn't real sure what was going on.''

When did Copeland notice this befuddlement on behalf of a senior quarterback with a record of 26-1? ``About the third series.''

Another moment. George Teague, tired, sore, poor George Teague, finds himself in the wrong place at the wrong time, watching Miami wideout Lamar Thomas' backside glide down the sideline. A minute before, Teague returned an interception for a touchdown for the first time in his life in his last college game, and his teammates pummeled him in celebration.

The very next Miami pass flies to a spot where Teague is not, to a man Teague can not catch. Not!

Some 82 yards from the snap, the burden switches from desperate feet to delicate hands. Teague, in the role of Harry Houdini, steals the ball from Thomas from behind on the dead run 7 yards from a Miami touchdown/wakeup call. ``I knew it was going to be my fault,'' Teague said, ``if I didn't hurry up and catch him.''

One more moment. Fourth quarter, fourth down at midfield, one inch short of an Alabama first down, one breath short of a Miami burial. Alabama coach Gene Stallings—button-down, heavy-on-the-starch Gene Stallings—turns and breathes the words, ``Go for it.'' They go for it. They get it. Miami breathes its last.

``I didn't feel we were the underdog,'' Stallings said of his 8 1/2-point underdog. ``Head-up, I thought we were the better football team. I say what I believe.'' Breathes there a man among us who no longer believes?

Heroes. You remember the Sugar Bowl in heroes. Tommy Johnson, a sophomore cornerback lost in the secondary shadows of Teague and Langham, breaks up more passes than a chaperone at a high-school dance. Johnson also intercepts a pass. Johnson also catches Lamar Thomas from behind and strips him of the ball in the Alabama end, making Thomas forever regret the pregame words, ``I think they should get out of their zone and be real men.''

Message for Mr. Thomas: Real men don't get caught from behind and stripped naked on national television. Real men, like Alabama guard George Wilson, shoot themselves in the foot but stand up like a man. Wilson and his fellow grunts at the front, Matt Hammond and Tobie Sheils and Jon Stevenson and Roosevelt Patterson, tear great, gaping holes in Miami's defensive reputation. Derrick Lassic runs through those holes and through Miami's suddenly unsure hands for 135 yards and the Most Valuable Player award.

Jay Barker passes for 18 yards, runs for 20 yards, runs his record as starting quarterback to 17-0. David Palmer finishes a season in purgatory with a long punt return to set up a field goal to open the scoring. Sam Shade intercepts a pass and sets the table for a touchdown. Bill Oliver proves beyond a shadow of a doubt that Bill Clinton erred by not naming Oliver secretary of defense.

When they dust the 1992 national championship trophy for fingerprints, they will find evidence implicating a lot more than the usual suspects.

``Just because they're good . . . ,'' Stallings said afterward, mistakenly using the present tense to describe Miami, `` . . . we're pretty good, too.'' Too modest, but too true.

For all the moments created by all the heroes, you remember the national championship for Mal Moore. Nobody on the field Friday night, not one player or coach on either sideline, has been a part of more national championships. Nobody on the field Friday night has been a part of so much winning and been a target of so much carping.

Mal-function. Moore is less. Offensive coordinator? Indeed. Offensive.

Funny. Miami's defense fancied itself the biggest and baddest in the land. Moore's offense, nothing fancy, pushed it around for 36 minutes of possession time. Funny. Alabama's defense outscored Miami's offense 7-6, but Moore's offense didn't need the help. Funny. Alabama has won a dozen national championships, and Moore has had a hand in seven of them.

``You can't believe how proud I am of this team and all the players,'' Moore said. ``I know how hard it is to do this, to win a national championship. You guys just imagine it in your minds.''

Twenty-three in a row . . . 13-0 . . . national champions . . . Alabama. Don't imagine it. Believe it.

Excited Alabama fans congratulate Jeremy Nunley and other Tide players after the game

The Sugar Bowl Play by Play

Alabama won the coin toss and elected to defer their choice to the second half. Miami elected to receive.

First quarter

Michael Proctor kicks off 65 yards to the Miami goal line; Kevin Williams returns for 18. George Teague makes the tackle.

First and 10: QB Gino Toretta passes to Donnell Bennett for 3. Sam Shades makes tackle.

Second and 7: Toretta from the shotgun is sacked for 3-yard loss by Tommy Johnson.

Third and 10: Toretta pass to Coleman Bell falls incomplete.

Fourth and 10: Paul Snyder punts for 44 yards to the Alabama 38. David Palmer returns to the Miami 38. Bennett makes the tackle.

First and 10 Alabama: Derrick Lassic up the middle for 4 to the Miami 20. Casey Greer makes tackle.

Second and 6: Lassic right for 14; pushed out of bounds at the Miami 6 by Jessie Armstead and Mark Caesar.

First and goal: Jay Barker pass to Lassic is tipped and incomplete.

Second and goal: Lassic right for three. Micheal Barrow makes tackle.

Third and goal: Barker back to pass; scrambles for 1. Robert Bass makes tackle.

Fourth and goal from the 2: Proctor kicks a 19 yard field goal with 10:56 remaining in the first quarter.

Proctor kicks off to the Miami goal line; Williams returns to the 21.

First and 10 Miami: Stephen McGuire up the middle for 1. James Gregory tackle.

Second and 9: Toretta passes to John Copeland for 5. Willie Gaston tackle.

Third and 4: Toretta passes to Williams for 34. Tommy Johnson tackle.

First and 10 at the Alabama 39: Toretta passes incomplete to Darryl Spencer.

Second and 10: Toretta passes to J. Harris for 10. Pushed out of bounds by Tommy Johnson.

First and 10 at the Alabama 29: McGuire loses three on a draw. Jeremy Nunley tackle.

Second and 13: Toretta passes incomplete to Williams.

Third and 13: Toretta passes incomplete to Lamar Thomas.

Fourth and 13: Dane Prewitt kicks 49-yard field goal.

Prewitt kicks off to the Alabama 9; David Palmer returns 17 yards and is pushed out of bounds by Malcolm Pearson on the 26.

First and 10 Alabama: Barker passes 6 yards to Prince Wimbley. Dexter Seigler tackle.

Second and 4: Lassic up the middle for 7. Terris Harris tackle.

First and 10: Lassic up the middle for 5. Kevin Patrick tackle.

Second and 5: Lassic up the middle for 4. Patrick tackle.

Third and 1: Lassic up the middle for 3. Greer tackle.

First and 10 at Miami 49: Barker passes incomplete to Chris Anderson.

Second and 10: Barker sacked for 6-yard loss by Rohan Marley and Barrow.

Third and 16: Barker intercepted by Greer at Miami 35; Greer runs out of bounds at the Alabama 39.

First and 10 Miami: Toretta passes to Bennett for 3. Derrick Oden and Antonio London tackle.

Second and 7: Toretta passes to Thomas for 13. Thomas stripped by Tommy Johnson; ball recovered by Willie Gaston at Alabama 23.

First and 10 Alabama: Lassic wide left, loses three. Caesar tackle.

Second and 13: Tarrant Lynch up middle for 12. Darrin Smith tackle.

Third and 1: Martin Houston left for 3. Armstead tackle.

First and 10 at Alabama 35: Lassic wide left for 7. Pushed out of bounds by Smith.

Second and 3: Barker back to pass; scrambled for

10. Lopez tackle.

First and 10 at Miami 48: Barker passes incomplete.

Second and 10: Barker passes incomplete to Lassic.

Third and 10: Barker intercepted by Ryan McNeil at the Miami 23, where he runs out of bounds.

First and 10 Miami: Toretta passes incomplete to Horace Copeland.

Second and 10: Williams on a reverse loses 8.

Third and 18: Toretta passes incomplete to Williams.

Fourth and 18: Snyder punts for 42 yards to the Alabama 43; Palmer returns 5 and Richardson makes the tackle.

First and 10 Alabama: Miami penalized 5 yards for offsides.

First and 5: Houston gets nothing on a draw. Darren Krein and Caesar tackle.

End of Quarter. **Alabama 3; Miami 3**

Second Quarter

Second and 5 Alabama: Lassic right for 24. Pushed out of bounds by T. Harris.

First and 10 at the Miami 23: Lassic up the middle for 1. Barrow tackle.

Second and 9: Barker left for 5. Smith and Barrow tackle.

Third and 4: Barker passes to Palmer for 6. Greer tackle.

First and 10 at the Miami 11: Lassic up the middle for 10. Riley tackle. Miami penalized 0 yards for face masking. Alabama penalized 15 yards for unsportsmanlike conduct (excessive celebration).

First and goal at Miami 16: Sherman Williams right for 4. Armstead and Greer tackle.

Second and 12: Williams up the middle for 8. Greer and Sapp tackle.

Third and 4: Lassic loses 2 up the middle. Caesar and Barrow tackle.

Fourth and 6: Proctor kicks a 23-yard field goal.

Proctor kicks off to the Miami goal line; Williams returns 28 yards. Teague makès the tackle.

First and 10 Miami: Toretta pass incomplete.

Second and 10: Toretta back to pass, scrambled for 15. Sam Shade and Eric Turner tackle.

First and 10 at the Miami 43: Bennett up the middle for 6. Gaston and Teague tackle.

Second and 4: Toretta loses 5 on a fumble and recovery.

Third and 9: Toretta pass intercepted by Shade at the Alabama 36. Shade returns 33 yards to the Miami 31. Toretta tackle.

First and 10 Alabama: Lassic right for 3. Greer tackle.

Second and 7: Lassic up the middle for 25. Armstead and Greer tackle.

First and goal at the Miami 3: Lassic right for 2. Krein tackle.

Second and goal: Lassic loses 1 up the middle. Barrow tackle.

Third and goal: Williams left for touchdown. Proctor kicks extra point.

Proctor kicks off to the Miami 6. Williams returns to the 31 where Johnson pushes him out of bounds.

First and 10 Miami: McGuire up the middle for 4. Copeland tackle.

Second and 6: McGuire loses 1 up the middle. Lemanski Hall and Copeland tackle.

Third and 7: Toretta passes incomplete to J. Harris. Broken up by Johnson.

Fourth and 7: Snyder punts 44 yards to the Alabama 22; Palmer loses a yard on the return.

First and 10 Alabama: Anderson wide right for 2. Greer tackle.

Second and 8: Lynch up the middle for 5. Riley tackle.

Third and 3: Anderson up the middle for no gain. Armstead tackle.

Fourth and 3: Bryne Diehl punts 57 yards to the Miami 15.

First and 10 Miami: Toretta passes incomplete to J. Harris.

Second and 10: Toretta passes to Thomas for 4. Shade tackle.

Third and 6: Toretta passes to Spencer for 8. Hall tackle.

First and 10 at the Miami 28: Miami penalized for

illegal procedure.

First and 15: Toretta passes to Ch. Jones for 9. Johnson and Hall tackle.

Second and 6: Toretta passes to Kevin Kirkeide for 14.

First and 10 at the Miami 46: Alabama penalized 5 yards for offsides.

First and 5: Toretta passes to Thomas for 6; pushed out of bounds by Chris Dannelly.

First and 10 at the Alabama 43: Toretta passes incomplete to Thomas; Gaston break up play.

Second and 10: Toretta passes incomplete to Williams. Langham breaks up play.

Third and 10: Toretta passes for 18 to Thomas. Gaston tackle.

First and 10 at the Alabama 25: Toretta passes incomplete.

Alabama calls consecutive time outs with one second remaining in the half.

Prewitt then kicks a 42-yard field goal.

End of half.

Alabama 13, Miami 6.

Third Quarter

Prewitt kicks off to the Alabama goal line; Williams returns to the 20.

First and 10 Alabama: Barker passes for 5 to Wimbley. McNeil and Armstead tackle.

Second and 5: Lassic up the middle for 2. Barrow tackle.

Third and 3: Barker passes incomplete to Palmer.

Fourth and 3: Diehl punts 44 yards to the Miami 29.

First and 10 Miami: Toretta's pass intercepted by Johnson at the Miami 43. Johnson returns 23 yards to the Miami 20. Williams tackle.

First and 10 Alabama: Lassic up the middle for no gain. Krein and Barrow tackle.

Second and 10: Lassic for 7 on a reverse. Greer tackle.

Third and 3: Barker back to pass; scrambles for 9. Riley tackle.

Miami penalized 2 yards for face masking.

First and goal from almost 2: Lassic up the middle for no gain. McNeil and Bass tackle.

Second and goal: Barker wide right for 1. Seigler tackle.

Third and goal: Lassic up the middle for touchdown.

Proctor kicks the extra point.

Alabama 20; Miami 6

Proctor kicks off to the Miami 6; Williams returns 23 yards. Michael Ausmus makes tackle

First and 10 Miami: Toretta pass intercepted by Teague at Miami 31. Teague returns for a touchdown.

Proctor kicks the extra point.

Alabama 27; Miami 6

Proctor kicks off to the Miami 1; Williams returns for 10. Ausmus makes the tackle.

First and 10 Miami: Bennett up the middle for no gain. Hall tackle.

Second and 10: Alabama penalized 5 yards for off

The National Championship

sides.

Second and 5: Toretta up the middle for 1. Nunley tackle.

Third and 4: Toretta passes incomplete to Copeland.

Fourth and 4: Snyder punts 41 yards to the Alabama 42; Palmer returns 7 yards. Smith tackle.

First and 10 Alabama: Houston up the middle for 14. T. Harris tackle.

First and 10: Williams loses 5 up the middle. Krein tackle.

Second and 15: Lassic up the middle for 2. Marley and Barrow tackle.

Third and 13: Barker passes to Lassic for a yard. Marley tackle.

Fourth and 12: Alabama penalized for delay of game.

Fourth and 17: Diehl punts 44 yards out of the end zone for a touchback.

First and 10 Miami: Toretta passes to Copeland for 16.

First and 10: Toretta passes incomplete to Bell.

Second and 10: Toretta passes to Bell for 34. Teague and Gaston tackle.

First and 10: Toretta passes incomplete to Bell. Broken up by Hall.

Second and 10: Toretta passes incomplete.

Third and 10: Toretta passes to Thomas for 6. Donnelly tackle.

Fourth and 4: Alabama penalized 5 yards for offsides.

First and 10: Toretta passes to Bennett for 4. Gaston tackle.

Second and 6: Bennett gets 4 on a draw to the Alabama 11. London and Donnelly tackle.

Third and 2: Toretta passes incomplete to Williams. Johnson breaks it up.

Fourth and 2: Toretta passes incomplete to Bell. Johnson breaks it up.

Ball goes to Alabama on downs at the Alabama 11 yard line.

First and 10 Alabama: Palmer gains 26 on a reverse. T. Harris tackle.

First and 10: Lassic loses 2 on a draw. Barrow tackle.

Second and 12: Lassic left for 2. Caesar and Krein tackle.

Third and 10: Barker passes incomplete to Wimbley.

Fourth and 10: Diehl punts 47 yards to the Miami 16. Williams returns 7 yards and runs out of bounds on the Miami 23.

End of quarter. **Alabama 27; Miami 6**

Fourth Quarter

First and 10 Miami: Toretta passes incomplete to Copeland.

Second and 10: Toretta passes incomplete to Spencer.

Third and 10: Toretta passes to Williams for 3. Oden tackle.

Fourth and 7: Snyder punts 37 yards to the Alabama 37; Palmer returns 3 yards.

First and 10 Alabama: Lynch up the middle for 4. Krein tackle.

Second and 6: Alabama penalized 5 yards for illegal procedure.

Second and 11: Lynch up the middle for 2. Riley and Caesar tackle.

Third and 9: Barker passes incomplete to Curtis Brown.

Fourth and 9: Diehl punts 37 yards to the Miami 22. Williams returns the punt 78 yards for a Miami touchdown.

Prewitt kicked the extra point.

Alabama 27; Miami 13

Prewitt kicked off to the Alabama 5. Palmer returned 36 yards and was pushed out of bounds by Marley at the Alabama 41.

First and 10 Alabama: Palmer loses 4 on a reverse. Barrow tackle.

Second and 14: Lassic runs left for 13. McNeil tackle.

Third and 1: Barker up the middle for no gain. Greer tackle.

Fourth and 1: Houston gains 1 up the middle.

First and 10: Lassic no gain. Barrow and Greer

Alabama fans must have known it would happen. They made the sign and brought it with them to the game.

tackle.

Second and 10: Houston for 2 up the middle. Marley tackle.

Third and 8: Miami penalized 15 yards for pass interference.

First and 10 at the Miami 32: Williams left for 6. Smith and Caesar tackle.

Second and 4: Williams up the middle for 3. Barrow tackle.

Third and 1: Houston right for 3. Patrick and Greer tackle.

First and 10 at the Miami 20: Lynch right for 16. Seigler tackle.

First and goal from the 4: Williams wide right for no gain. Bass pushes him out of bounds.

Second and goal: Lassic wide left for touchdown. Proctor kicks the extra point.

Proctor kicks off to the Miami goal line. Williams returns to the 21 where he runs out of bounds.

First and 10 Miami: Miami penalized 10 yards for personal foul.

First and 20: Toretta passes for 7 to Bennett. London tackle.

Second and 13: Toretta passes incomplete to Copeland.

Third and 13: Toretta passes to Williams for 12; pushed out of bounds by Gaston.

Fourth and 1: Bennett left for 2. Copeland tackle.

First and 10: Toretta passes incomplete to Ch. Jones.

Second and 10: Toretta passes to Ch. Jones for 15. Teague tackle.

First and 10: Toretta passes incomplete.

Second and 10: Toretta passes to Thomas for 5. Gaston tackle.

Third and 5: Toretta loses 7 up the middle, fumbles, but recovers at his 45.

Fourth and 12: Toretta passes incomplete to Williams.

Alabama gets the ball on downs.

First and 10 Alabama at the Miami 45: Anderson wide right for 2. Smith and Pearson tackle.

Second and 8: Anderson no gain. Sapp tackle.

Third and 8: Burgdorf up the middle for 6. Armstead tackle.

Fourth and 2: Alabama penalized for delay of game.

Fourth and 8: Diehl punts for 38 yards. Ball is downed at the Miami 5.

First and 10 Miami at its 5: Bennett up the middle for 16. Donnelley tackle.

First and 10: Toretta passes to J. Harris for 6. ; Runs out of bounds at the Miami 27.

Second and 4: Toretta passes incomplete. Shade breaks up pass.

Third and 4: L. Jones gains 8 on a draw. Turner and E. Brown make tackle.

First and 10: Toretta passes incomplete to Thomas.

Second and 10: Toretta passes to L. Jones for 3. Donnelly tackle.

Third and 7: Toretta passes to Ch. Jones for 40 to the Alabama 9. Langham tackle.

First and goal: L. Jones right for 5. Oden tackle.

Second and goal: Toretta passes incomplete to Ch. Jones. Langham breaks it up.

Third and goal: Toretta passes incomplete to Ch. Jones.

End of game.

Alabama 34; Miami 13

The Season

Spring training revealed both problems and promise

Hopeful Beginnings

Preseason Training

The April 12 *Birmingham News* reported Alabama's centennial celebration, team of the century selections, stories of old grads and of national championships revisited.

It reported that the performance of backup quarterbacks Brian Burgdorf and Chad Key highlighted the A-Day game which, incidentally, was won 13-7 by the White team led by Key and, briefly, starting quarterback Jay Barker.

The game drew 35,000, more to see the old stars, gather autographs and enjoy a concert by the band Alabama during the all-day festivities marking the 100th years that the University of Alabama has fielded a football team.

Gary Rutledge, a wishbone quarterback from the 70s, won the Centennial Quarterback Throw.

Robert Stewart, John Sullins, Siran Stacy and Kevin Turner—stars from the 1991 Alabama team—mashed their hands and feet into wet cement at Denny

Chimes as permanent captains of the 1991 team.

Walk-on linebacker Thad Turnipseed was the sole player injured in the spring game, suffering a significant knee injury.

And, finally, in the sixth and final item in a column rounding up the odds and ends of the day was a note about Jeremy Nunley winning the Dixie Howell Memorial Award as the A-Day game's most valuable player.

He offered several typical words of thanks, not unlike the dozens before him, but which on January 1, 1993, prove quite prophetic: "The important thing is that we improved this spring as a team. You could tell everybody was real competitive...which can only make us a better team this fall.

"We have a real shot at being No. 1 this fall, and that's what we're working toward."

Fast forward four months to Tuesday, August 11. First day of fall drills. Staff writer Charles Hollis got the first inkling of things to come:

TUSCALOOSA—On the first day of fall practice, Alabama coach Gene Stallings saw a bunch of things he liked.

Three things in particular stood out:

• The general physical condition of the team. Not just players with trimmed-down bodies, but players with more quickness and endurance than in the past.

• The quarterbacking of Jay Barker, Brian Burgdorf and Chad Key.

• The way the players approached Tuesday's first day on the practice field.

"I thought we went right to work...it was sort of like we picked up where we left off in spring practice. That wasn't the case the last two years," Stallings said after the second of two long workouts in shorts and helmets.

The players conditioning during the off season was apparent to Stallings. "There were a few out there who weren't in shape, but overall I thought the team came back in pretty good shape," he said.

As for starting QB Barker, Stallings said it was obvious the 6-foot-3, 205-pound sophomore from Trussville had made good use of the off season. "You couldn't help but notice Jay out there," he said.

Senior fullback Martin Houston, a fifth-year senior and one of the trimmed-down bodies, said he noticed it immediately.

"This is a more experienced team and you could see it today," he said. "We just continued where we left off in the spring. I think part of that was the way everybody came back in shape.

"I think this is the best shape of any team I've seen in the fall in my five years here."

"I'm weighing 230 pounds, the lightest I've ever been. I played last season at 235 and above. Mostly above.

"During our running tests yesterday, I made all eight 220s. I've never done that before. Last week I made only five 220s. By the grace of God and guts, I finally made my running tests in my last year."

A total of 144 players participated in the start of fall drills, including about 60 walk-ons. Since spring practice ended in April, the Tide has placed at least four players on scholarship: quarterback Key of Jasper, snapper/tight end Matthew Pine of Gadsden, holder/cornerback Jeff Wall and junior college signee Dennis Deason, both of Vestavia Hills.

For a first day, added Stallings, "It wasn't bad at all. I was pleased for the most part. I don't want to mention a lot of names right now, but I couldn't help but notice some players who've worked hard this summer...who look pretty good to me.

The Crimson Tide defense, which is expected to be one of the best in the nation, had several veterans who stood out on the first day, including ends John Copeland and Eric Curry, linebacker Derrick Oden, outside linebackers Antonio London and Lemanski Hall and cornerback/safety George Teague.

Teague, a senior, spent most of his time Tuesday playing cornerback while sophomore Sam Shade and junior Chris Donnelly handled the safeties.

"We're working George at both corner and free safety," said Stallings. "He'll probably play both positions. But we have some other players, especially some young players, who could help us."

Two newcomers have already made an impression in the secondary. Freshman Blair Canale and Willie Gaston, who sat out the 1991 season as a Proposition 48 player, are showing signs they could help.

"We may not have 12 true freshmen play like we did last year, but we've got several who might," said Stallings. "But it's a lot different trying to play for a team that needs help (from the freshman class) than it is for a team that doesn't."

Two days later there were more encouraging signs from fall practice. Hollis filed this piece on the Alabama offensive line:

TUSCALOOSA, August 14—William Barger of Birmingham, the second-team right guard behind Jon Stevenson, had a history of failing to run fast enough to impress Alabama coaches when fall football practice started.

But thanks to a $50 bet from left offensive guard John Clay, Barger made his time and has some extra pocket money.

"Barger's never made his times before," said offensive line coach Jim Fuller. "And I don't think he would have made them this year if they hadn't bet each other.

"I can't say whether Clay's going to pay off. But Barger sure surprised the heck out of me by making his times."

The conditioning tests and the first three days of fall practice have been surprising in another way to Fuller.

For the first time in years, Fuller said Alabama has linemen that look and move like linemen "are supposed to at Alabama. I don't have to go too far back...to remember how lean times were."

With virtually every player returning on the two-deep chart, Alabama is expected to field its most experienced line in years.

Fuller said it wouldn't surprise him "if I don't become a better coach" now.

Coaches seemed equally pleased with the running talent of halfback Derrick Lassic, but worried whether the injury-prone player could go the distance. Hollis found that the issue worried the Haverstraw, N.Y., runner as well.

TUSCALOOSA, August 16—Go ahead and say it. Everybody else does. Derrick Lassic is prone to injury.

"I started to shake it last year, but I still hear, 'When you going to get hurt, Lassic?' said the fifth-year running back.

Since his redshirt year in 1988, injuries have slowed Lassic's progress.

"I see no reason why Derrick shouldn't excel this year," said running back coach Larry Kirksey. "We know he can play. He's a very gifted athlete who runs wide-open on every play. And we've also discovered he runs excellent pass routes."

Because of Lassic's reputation for pulling something or bruising something, he has had a hard time being full speed for every game.

"Last year I was able to play every game, even when I got the hip-pointer late in the year," said Lassic. "I've at least learned how to play with pain.

"If I'd had the hip-pointer my sophomore year, I would have been out for one or two games."

When Alabama opens the season Sept. 5 against Vanderbilt, it will be his first start.

A healthy Lassic could mean an even more dangerous runner than (Siran) Stacy (Alabama's 1991 star running back). Lassic is faster with his 4.4 speed, stronger with his 330-pound bench press and more explosive to the line of scrimmage.

"We do have some talent at running back, starting with Derrick," added Kirksey. "It is a good situation when Derrick knows he can go out and give everything he has, then turn it over to

Jim Fuller says he thinks the 1992 offensive line may make him a better coach

Chris Anderson or Sherman Williams. Those are two speeders."

An omen of things to come.

Alabama's first pre-season scrimmage was August 15 and Stallings had praise for the offense, with Jay Barker hitting 10 of 18 passes for 176 yards and two touchdowns. The young quarterback said it was just what he needed to let his teammates know "they can have confidence in me."

David Palmer snared two passes for 100 yards; Prince Wimbley caught a touchdown pass and a green kicker, freshman Michael Proctor, knocked home a 51-yard field goal that could have been good at close to 60.

Meanwhile, coach Bill Oliver fretted over not enough players in the defensive backfield:

TUSCALOOSA, August 20—It is not unusual to see the Crimson Tide use six and seven defensive backs, depending on the opponent, down and situation.

And when you least expect the Tide to blitz, here comes a cornerback cheating up on the line of scrimmage, ready to disrupt any action in the backfield.

It is all part of Bill Oliver's reputation as one of the top secondary coaches in college football.

Unless help arrives soon, Oliver may not have enough defensive backs to use in his chess games with the opposing team's offense.

"We're thin in numbers," said Oliver.

To play the coverages he likes to play, to have enough depth to make it work, Oliver said he could use two more players.

"We have five people we feel we can put on the field and win with," said Oliver. "We have George Teague, Antonio Langham, Chris Donnelly, Sam Shade and Tommy Johnson. Those five are football players. But if we had war anywhere in the world, I'd be happy to go to war with just those five."

And so the shuffling went. Young players like Will Brown and Andre Royal forging forward, only for Royal to go down to injury later; Willie Gaston working into the secondary and freshman defensive back Blair Canale impressing coaches until suffering a season-ending knee injury two weeks before the opener.

On August 23, the Associated Press released its first college football poll. The University of Miami was ranked number one. Alabama was ranked ninth. Consensus was that with a stronger team than 1991 and what appeared to be a soft schedule, Alabama should have as good a season as last year and win the western division of the Southeastern Conference—say 11-1, or maybe 10-2 with a bit of bad luck.

The annual predictions at that time by *The News* sports staff went this way:

The Road to No. 1

Five games that will decide the national championship.
1. Michigan at Notre Dame, Sept. 12.
2. Miami at Penn State, Oct. 10.
3. Penn State at Notre Dame, Nov. 14.
4. Miami at Syracuse, Nov. 21.
5. Florida at Alabama, Dec. 5.

12 (or 13) and Oh

Talent, schedule, luck. Five teams that have the groundwork to go undefeated.
1. Alabama.
2. Notre Dame.
3. Penn State.
4. Syracuse.
5. Texas A&M.

More road to No. 1

Top 10 reasons Alabama could, maybe, perhaps contend for a national championship.
1. John Copeland, Eric Curry and company on defense.
2. The team's best and deepest offensive line in years.
3. Siran Stacy was the only person who could stop tailback Derrick Lassic.
4. David Palmer is the only person who can stop

David Palmer.

    5. Gene Stallings will keep the pressure off.

    6. Florida is off the schedule.

    7. Georgia is off the schedule.

    8. The Tide plays just three teams that had winning records last season.

    9. The Tide plays Auburn in Legion Field.

    10. In the 100th season of Alabama football, the Bear would want it that way.

There was great confidence in a good season, but only shaky hope for a spectacular one. There seemed to be no corner of doubt about a defense that would keep Alabama in the toughest of games. But the offense was another question, with the largest question of all on a sophomore quarterback who seemed capable of little—except winning.

Tide's Barker the new kid on the block;
Soph QB has only 4 starts, but has led Bama to 4 wins

By Charles Hollis

TUSCALOOSA, August 23—There is something about Alabama quarterback Jay Barker that makes you feel good the moment you meet him.

It's hard to say why Barker is like that.

It might be how he goes out of his way to let you know he isn't anyone special.

He might seem a little quiet and shy at first, but that usually goes away after a handshake and a hello. Once he warms up, once the ice is broken, the 6-foot-3, 210-pound sophomore is going to rock you with how polite and down to earth he is.

A big part of it is his faith in God. Church is important to Barker. And church is commitment, just like football. "I look at my situation, and I really mean this...I feel the Lord has blessed me with a platform to carry His word and the opportunity to perform on the field."

If a church group asks him to come and talk to young people, and if he can find the time between school and football, he'll be there.

"I'm aware there are so many guys around who talk about the Lord and try to push their faith on you, but I'm not going to do that.

"I don't want to turn off people with some holier than thou attitude. You can preach by example," he added.

And there is Barker's work ethic. Whether it's the off season or after practice, Barker is almost always the last one to leave. Each day during two-a-days, Barker would run sprints with his teammates and when practice was over, he would either stay late and work on his throwing or do extra running.

"The quarterback has got to set the tempo," said Barker. "If guys see the quarterback taking it easy, if they see he's not working as hard as they are, they're going to notice.

"I've got to be in the best shape of anybody on the team. I want to win every sprint in my group. I've got to go out every day and prove myself. If the other players think you're tired, they're going to have doubts in the huddle on a long drive. I want them to have complete confidence in me."

You can't help but wonder if Barker is for real. There is a similar correlation with Barker and the starting job he holds.

Barker has started only four games for Alabama. But he is 4-0 as the starter and that helped the Crimson Tide go 11-1 last season.

Against Colorado in the Blockbuster Bowl, a 30-25 Alabama victory, Barker played his best game. He threw three touchdown passes, all coming on third-down plays.

"A game like that can make all the difference in your confidence," said coach Gene Stallings. "You could see how much it did for Jay's confidence in the spring. And this fall, he's performing like a starting quarterback is supposed to by the way he is handling the offense."

But the fact remains the Sept. 5 opener against Vanderbilt will be Barker's fifth start. And unlike last year when Barker and Danny Woodson dueled for the starting job on a team that wasn't picked high in the polls, this year the Crimson Tide is ranked among the top teams in college football.

Barker knows Tide fans are expecting the Barker they saw against Colorado. He knows they have seen him on the cover of preseason magazines and they

Jay Barker just *seems* like your average guy

hope he is for real.

"I think there is a feeling that if the quarterback position comes through, everything else will fall into place," said Barker, who didn't play quarterback until his last year at Hewitt-Trussville. "I can understand that. Our defense should be outstanding. The kicking game should be better. And when you look at our offense and see the talent we have at wide receiver, at running back and the experience we have in the offensive line, you've got to be excited about the possibilities we have on offense.

"I feel fortunate to have players like we have around me. A lot of times you hear that quarterbacks are told they can't make mistakes and not to do this in this situation, or run this play in another situation. It's true.

"I feel the Lord has blessed me with enough talent to be a successful quarterback. I've just got to rely on that talent to make sure I don't get us beat."

Barker knew there was going to be attention directed his way this year as the No. 1 QB. He said it went with the position and the Alabama program, which has produced players such as Bart Starr, Joe Namath, Kenny Stabler, Richard Todd and Jeff Rutledge.

Yet he wasn't expecting to see himself on the cover of so many preseason publications.

Barker was at the beach last month in Panama City with his family and girlfriend, when he saw his picture on the cover for the first time.

"I have to admit I bought it," he said, laughing. "And I have to admit I like the attention. I'd by lying if I said I didn't."

But he said he hasn't bought into the hype "I'm some great quarterback, because I'm not. Like Coach Stallings said earlier this summer, I've really just played in five games and started four. I haven't proven anything.

"This is really my first season as the No. 1 quarterback. Week in and week out, it's going to be a constant process of trying to get better—trying not to make the same mistakes I made the week before."

One part of his game he knew he had to improve over last years was his passing, especially where the ball went and how fast it got there.

"His accuracy is so much better," said Brian Burgdorf, who is battling Chad Key for the backup spot. "But the real improvement I've noticed is the zip he has on the ball. Jay is throwing the ball so much harder than he was in the spring."

To Barker, a successful quarterback is more than touchdown passes and wins. "It's being a leader and earning the respect of your teammates on and off the field.

"You can't do that by talking about it. You do it with hard work—by example."

Season at Hand

The season was at hand. Stallings would ride with his lightly-tested quarterback, and experienced line, talented runners and receivers and one of the most promising defenses ever assembled at the Capstone.

46

The coach was uneasy, grouchy. After three scrimmages and 21 practices in 12 days, Stallings pronounced the team needing more work. In an 87-play scrimmage the defense put Barker on his back twice in the first quarter, and intercepted a pass.

Stallings criticized the offensive line for not providing decent protection.

"I think we're making progress, but I still worry about the inexperience we have in some places," said Stallings. "Nobody works harder than Jay Barker, but the fact is he has started only four games.

"And behind Jay we've got Brian Burgdorf and Chad Key. They're working hard, but they haven't played in a game."

He also fretted about young Michael Proctor. "The pressure, the intensity, the size of the people he'll kick against (this fall), those are big changes for him."

Proctor had a mild groin pull and the coach worried that he would not be able to handle kickoffs. He lamented the loss of Blair Canale from the already thin secondary, and the lack of a backup at tight end. Maybe redshirt freshman Tony Johnson could do it, or maybe freshman Kris Mangum, even though he wanted to give Mangum a redshirt year.

He fiddled with linebacker, switching Mario Morris and Michael Rogers, then switching them back.

Freshman runner Eric Turner moved to defensive back and quickly began working his way up the depth chart.

The shuffling may have continued, but for the calendar. September 5 had arrived and at 11:40 a.m. in Bryant-Denny Stadium a true freshman from Pelham, Michael Proctor, kicked the University of Alabama Crimson Tide into its 100th season of football.

An auspicious beginning for freshman Michael Proctor, booting four field goals in his first collegiate game

A Modest Start

Vanderbilt

Alabama Passes First Test

By Charles Hollis

TUSCALOOSA—The timing was perfect for the debut of Alabama's new and improved passing offense.

After two years of run, run, run under coach Gene Stallings, the Crimson Tide picked the first game of its centennial year of football to feature the pass. With Vanderbilt's game plan designed to stop the run and force Alabama to throw, the ninth-ranked Crimson Tide played right into the Commodores' hands for a 25-8 season-opening victory before a capacity crowd of 70,123 at Bryant-Denny Stadium Saturday.

When the Alabama defense forced the first of five first-half Vanderbilt turnovers on the Commodores' opening drive, which reached the Alabama 17, the offense took over and quarterback Jay Barker quickly found himself looking at an eight-man front.

Vandy was in a 4-3 defense, not the 3-4 the tide had worked against in practice.

"We could see real quick they were not going to let us beat them with our running game," said Barker, making his 1992 debut as the starting quarterback. "They were daring us to throw the football."

And Barker threw. Twenty-seven times he threw, which was seven more times than Alabama threw in any game last season. Barker completed 14, tying the most completions of any game last year, and he threw one interception.

His passing yardage: 185. The running game: 104.

"I wonder how long has it's been since an Alabama team has thrown more than we've run the ball? But Vanderbilt came out with eight and nine guys on the line and just dared us to throw it," said senior running back Derrick Lassic, the game's leading rusher with 51 yards on 9 carries.

The passing yardage was also accomplished without star receiver David Palmer, who was sitting out a one-game suspension for his drunk driving charge over the summer.

"You know it was a tough decision for coach Stallings to make," said senior wide receiver Prince Wimbley, "but this shows what the other receivers can do.

"We have other people who can make plays besides David. But David means a lot to this team, and he was a one-man cheerleader for the rest of us."

After Lassic burned the Vanderbilt defense for a 36-yard gain of the first play, Barker proceeded to hit his first two passes and put freshman Michael Proctor in position to kick the first of his four field goals.

When the first quarter ended, Proctor had converted from 46, 43 and 42 yards to give Alabama a 9-0 lead. He added a 32-yarder in the fourth quarter to set a freshman record with four field goals.

"We were expecting a lot from Michael Proctor, but even did better than I was expecting," said Stallings. "He did and outstanding job."

As for the passing game, Stallings thought it played a big role in Alabama winning, especially late when the Tide was backed up on its 6-yard line and clinging to a 16-8 lead.

Barker directed the offense on it longest drive of the game at that point, a 12-play, 80-yard march that ended with Proctor's 32-yard field goal.

"We still have to improve on the passing game,

TOP 25 AP POLL
1. MIAMI
2. WASHINGTON
3. NOTRE DAME
4. FLORIDA
5. FLORIDA STATE
6. MICHIGAN
7. TEXAS A7M
8. ALABAMA
9. SYRACUSE
10. PENN STATE
11. NEBRASKA
12. COLORADO
13. OKLAHOMA
14. GEORGIA
15. CLEMSON
16. UCLA
17. CALIFORNIA
18. MISSISSIPPI STATE
19. NORTH CAROLINA STATE
20. TENNESSEE
21. STANFORD
22. OHIO STATE
23. VIRGINIA
24. GEORGIA TECH
25. BYU

but we did some things better than last year," said assistant head coach Mal Moore, who calls much of the offense from the sideline. "I thought Jay was spectacular for the first game out this year. I thought he threw the ball better today than he did last year."

Alabama's lone drive followed Vandy's only scoring drive of the game. The Commodores had taken the second half kickoff to pull within 16-8 after three quarters.

Proctor's field goal gave the Tide a 19-8 lead and some breathing room.

"When they got within eight points and we had to play a little tougher, I think our players did," said Stallings. "I thought we responded the way a team is supposed to. I thought Jay Barker responded well.

"Jay made some throws ... some timely throws. And our defense came up with some big plays when in counted. It feels good to open up with a win."

It didn't feel good to Vanderbilt coach Gerry DiNardo, who said he felt his team-a 22 point underdog-could come into Tuscaloosa and pull the upset.

"We had to have a near perfect game and we didn't have one," said DiNardo, whose team committed seven turnovers in the game, four fumbles and three interceptions. "The five turnovers we had the first half hurt us alot, but our defense held them to three field goals. That's progress."

At the half, DiNardo said he told his team "to play well in the second half. We didn't want to be routed. Those days are over.

"It's hard to believe we'll see a better defense than Alabama's. Their defense is very good."

The Crimson Tide defense was everything it was built up to be, and didn't waste time doing it. On Vandy's first eight possession, the Tide forced five turnovers and stopped another drive when Willis Bevelle tackled punter David Lawrence deep in his territory.

Perhaps the biggest play by the Alabama defense came on Vandy's opening drive, after the Commodores caught the Tide by surprise with a fake punt.

Facing fourth-and-four at the Alabama 42,

Lawrence dropped back to punt, but instead passed to a wide-open Robert Davis down the sideline for 41 yards.

But with first down at the Alabama 17, the defense came up with the first of its five first-half turnovers. End John Copeland stripped the ball away from fullback Carlos Thomas at the line of scrimmage and linebacker Lemanski Hall pounced on it at the 15.

From there, the Tide drove to the first Proctor field goal.

While Vandy had trouble hanging onto the ball, the Tide was having just as much trouble getting into the end zone. Its only offensive touchdown, a 6-yard run by Lassic, was set Bevelle's tackle of Lawrence at the Vandy 6 early in the second quarter.

Lassic scored on the first play. Proctor's kick made it 16-0 with 11 minutes to go in the half.

Neither offense did any real damage in the first half. The Tide managed only seven first downs and 156 total yards, with 87 of that through the air. Vandy had nine first downs and 143 yards out of its I-Bone.

Alabama had two opportunities to add to its lead, but Barker turned the ball over both times. He threw an interception at the Vandy 11 after the Tide had moved to the 28, and he lost the ball at the Vandy 13 when a Commodore knocked the ball out of his hands.

The Tide offense simply couldn't sustain a long drive through the first three quarters. In fact, it didn't have a third-down conversion until the last two minutes of the third quarter. Barker hooked up with Lassic out of the backfield for 19 yards for a first down at the Alabama 37.

After Vanderbilt took the second half kickoff and drove for its first points, a 4-yard touchdown by fullback Royce Love with eight minutes to go in the third period, the defense took it from there.

"We had just got whipped up and down the field on that drive," said Tide linebacker Michael Rogers,

Chris Anderson provides some of Alabama's offense in opening Vandy game

who returned an interception 36 yards for a touchdown with 1:50 remaining.

"That opened our eyes."

Alabama continued its domination of Vanderbilt with the win. The Tide has won eight in a row against its Southeastern Conference rival and 30 of 32 since 1960.

Stallings sees good and bad in opener

By Charles Hollis

TUSCALOOSA-For the first time out this year, Alabama coach Gene Stallings thought his football team handled itself well.

Even though there were some rough spots, especially with the running game and the run defense, Stallings said he liked the effort, the kicking game and the 25-8 victory Saturday over the Vanderbilt Commodores.

"It was good to open up with a win," he said. "It's not a lot of fun when you don't start out with a victory."

And Stallings said winning without his star player, wide receiver/kick returner David Palmer, made the rough spots easier to live with. "Because there were going to be a lot of second guessing by our fans and you guys (in the media) over my decision not to let David play," he said.

"I know I left myself open for criticism, but I made the decision a month and a half ago and I did it in the best interest of David Palmer. If we had lost, you would be writing how my decision cost us the game.

"Sometimes you have to look at the situation and decide what is best for the individual and the team," added Stallings. "I felt it was pretty severe punishment, but now it's over. David will be back next week and as far as I'm concerned, that's the end of it.

"For someone who loves to win as much as David does, for someone who loves to compete as much as David does, you better believe this hurt David to have to miss the first game of the season."

Stallings will now worry about smoothing the kinks out of an offense that compiled more yards passing (185) than running (148), a little different for a Stallings team.

"It probably was a shock to our fans to see us throw the ball as much as we did," said sophomore quarterback Jay Barker. "They're not used to seeing us pass more than we run."

But that was by design in some ways, Stallings said.

With Vanderbilt springing a new defense on the

Tide, using a 4-3 instead of its usual 3-4, the Commodores made the decision to shut down the run and make Alabama beat them with the pass.

"We were not looking for that defense," Stallings said. "But I thought that Jay handled himself pretty good. He made some throws. There were some times when I'm sure Jay wished he could have had the play back, but for the most part I was pleased with the way Jay played."

Barker completed 14 of 27 passes for 185 yards. He also threw an interception at the Vanderbilt 11-yard line and a Vandy defender forced Barker to fumble as he was about to pass.

"I was looking for improvement in our passing game," said Stallings. "That's the thing we've got to improve on. I thought we did some things better than we did last year.

"I thought our kicking game was outstanding. For his first game, (freshman) Michael Proctor did an outstanding job. The thing that bothered me was the first half when we had five turnovers (from Vandy) and got only 16 points. If I were in that other dressing room, I'd think I'd played pretty well."

One thing Stallings liked a lot were the penalties: only three for 15 yards. "That's better than last year when we would jump offside, fumble the snap, get a hold or do something to stop a drive."

There were not may memorable drives against Vandy. It wasn't until late in the third quarter when the Crimson Tide finally converted on third down.

But when Vanderbilt cut the score to 16-8 after three quarters, and with the suspense back in the game, Stallings said the offense took the ball at its own five-yard line and drove for a field goal.

"When they got within eight and we had to play a little tougher, I think our players did. I thought they responded to it pretty well," said Stallings.

Alabama did it with the pass. "That was good to see, but our running game has to be more productive than (148 yards for the game)," Stallings continued.

His defense, he liked a lot. With the exception of Vandy's second-half drive that hurt the defense with inside running plays, Stallings was satisfied with the effort.

"I think our defense is going to be pretty good," he said. "But give Vanderbilt credit for that drive ... and No. 2 (quarterback Marcus Wilson). He made some clutch plays against us.

"I said earlier this week this was going to be a tight game, and it went about like I thought."

That is, except for a surprise fake punt of Vandy's first possession. When punter David Lawrence fired a 41-yard pass to Robert Davis on fourth-and-four at the Alabama 42, that caught the Tide sideline by surprise.

"I didn't expect to see that," Stallings said. "That's my fault. We should have been ready for something like that."

GAME STATS AND SCORING

Alabama	9	7	0	9	25
Vanderbilt	0	0	8	0	8

STATISTICS	UA	VU
First Downs	15	15
Rushing (Atts/Yds)	34-104	61-138
Passing (Comp/Atts/Int)	14-27-1	4-15-3
Passing Yards	185	72
Total Offense	289	210
Average Gain Per Play	4.74	2.76
Fumbles/Lost	3-1	4-3
Total Turnovers	2	6
Punting(No/Avg)	3-36.2	5-46.2
Punt Returns(No/Yds)	4-32	1-15
Kickoff Returns(No/Yds)	1-17	6-140
Penalties/Yards	3-15	4-35
Time of Possession	24:46	35:14
Third Down Conversions	3-13	6-17
Fourth Down Conversions	0-0	1-2
Sacks/Lost	6-29	4-34

INDIVIDUAL STATISTICS

Rushing (Att-Yds-TD): UA—Lassic 9-51-1; Houston 10-49-0; Anderson 2-19-0; Wimbley 1-(-2)-0; Lynch 3-15-0; Harris 2-2-0; Barker 6-(-28)-0; Burgdorf 1-(-2)-0.
VU—Wilson 24-32-0; Jackson 16-44-0; Thomas 6-20-0; E. Lewis 8-37-0; Lawrence 1-(-1)-0; Weir 1-(-7)-0; Love 5-13-1.

Passing (Comp-Att-I-Yds-TD): UA—Barker 14-27-1-185-0
VU—Lawrence 1-1-0-41-0; Wilson 3-14-3-31-0.

Receiving (Rec-Yds-TD): UA—Wimbley 2-28-0; Lee 3-78-0; Lassic 3-29-0; C. Brown 2-23-0; Busky 2-17-0; Houston 1-2-0; Anderson 1-8-0
VU—Davis 1-41-0; Jackson 1-10-0; Sevillian 1-19-0; Love 1-2-0.

DEFENSIVE STATISTICS

Tackles (Primary-Assists-Total): UA—Copeland 8-4-12; Oden 6-6-12; London 7-4-11; Gregory 3-4-7; Rogers 6-0-6; Curry 3-3-6; Morris 2-4-6; Donnelly 4-2-6.
VU—Quarles 6-3-9; Brothers 6-3-9; B. Davis 6-1-7; A. Smith 4-2-6; Francis 3-3-6; Collins 5-1-6.

Sacks: UA—Nunley 2 (-12); Copeland 1 (-6); Roger 1 (-5).
VU—Quarles 1 (-13); DeWitt 1 (-8); Cates 1 (-7).

Tackles for Losses: UA—Hall 2 (-4); Copeland 2 (-2); London 1 (-7).
VU—Melton 1 (-3); Quarles 1 (-2); Collins 1 (-1).

Passes Broken Up: UA—London 1. VU-Francis 1.

Interceptions: UA—Rogers. Langham, Donnelly (1 each).
VU—A. Smith 1.

Fumbles Recovered: UA—Hall 2; Shade 1. VU-Francis 1.

Fumbles Caused: UA—Copeland 2. VU-Francis 1.

Quarterback Pressures: UA—Copeland, Morris, Nunley (1 each).
VU—Francis, Manley (1 each).

SCORING SUMMARY

First Quarter
UA 3, VU 0—8:17 Michael Proctor 46-yard field goal [9 plays, 57 yards, 2:56]
UA 6, VU 0—7:03 Proctor 43-yard field goal [4 plays, -1 yard, 0:56]
UA 9, VU 0—2:21 Proctor 42-yard field goal [6 plays, 50 yards, 2:04]

Second Quarter
UA 16, VU 0—11:01 Derrick Lassic 4-yard run (Proctor kick) [2 plays, 6 yards, 0:48]

Third Quarter
UA 16, VU 8—7:53 Royce Love 5-yard run (Eric Lewis run) [14 plays, 53 yards, 7:07]

Fourth Quarter
UA 19, VU 8—7:42 Proctor 32-yard field goal [12 plays, 80 yards, 5:21]
UA 25, VU 8—1:59 Michael Rogers 36-yard int. return (PAT blocked)

54

Michael Rogers, Alabama player top right, and cohorts smother Southern Miss' offense

Too Close For Comfort
Southern Mississippi

Tide defense strangles USM

By Jimmy Bryan

BIRMINGHAM, September 13—The Alabama defense draped a curtain of Crimson Steel around Legion Field Saturday and beat Southern Mississippi 17-10.

The Crimson Tide offense might as well have stayed home.

The defense took charge on Southern Miss' first series when it threw the Golden Eagle offense for three straight losses. It stayed in charge until corner-back Antonio Langham intercepted a pass on the Golden Eagles' final offensive play with 1.25 left in the game.

Thirteen times the Crimson Steel Curtain battered the Southern Mississippi offense for negative yardage. Remember the names of Eric Curry, John Copeland, Lemanski Hall, Antonio London, Tommy Johnson, Sam Shade, James Gregory, Derrick Oden, Antonio Langham and Jeremy Nunley. They can play defense. For the game, the Golden Eagles had 28 yards rushing on 27 attempts, 26 yards passing on 7-of-19 and produced only three first downs—two by rushing and one by penalty. The Tide tied a school record by allowing no first downs passing.

The Southern Mississippi offense didn't come

close to producing a touchdown. The Golden Eagles' only touchdown was a gift from the Alabama offense, an 18-yard interception return by defensive end Bobby Hamilton that tied the game 7-7.

Southern Miss later cashed a fumble recovery at the Alabama 18 into a go-ahead field goal. But the Eagles got nothing from their offense even after the recovery, netting only 3 yards in three plays, and were forced to settle for the field goal.

Alabama's special teams, an affiliate of the defense, scored the first touchdown of the game on a 73-yard scoring pass off a fake punt. The special teams set up the Tide's field goal by recovering a fumbled punt at the Southern Miss 20.

The offense got untracked for one successful drive, a 63-yard march in 10 fourth-quarter plays for the winning touchdown.

"We had a lot of distractions this week," Alabama coach Gene Stallings said. "It's hard for the general public to realize (the impact these distractions made). I know it affected me.

"We had what was going on with David Palmer (charged with his second DUI infraction) and Ralph Thompson (Georgia defensive back who accused the Tide of illegal recruiting). And then (offensive guard) Jon Stevenson's brother getting killed in a fighter plane.

"A lot of things bothered us. Penalties really hurt. It seemed every time we started doing something, we'd lose that, plus 15 more yards in penalties."
Alabama had 383 yards offense to just 54 for USM, and both were hurt by penalties. The Tide was penalized nine times for 78 yards, the Eagles 10 for 81. Also, Alabama fumbled six times and lost two.
"The best thing about it was that we won," said Stallings. "The bad thing was we had too many major penalties."

Southern Miss coach Jeff Bower said, "Our defense kept us in the game. We didn't do anything offensively. In fact, we were physically manhandled. I'm very disappointed in our offense. We couldn't even run the draw."

The Crimson Tide shocked Southern Mississippi

with a big gamble on its first offensive series. Faced with fourth-and-eight from its 27, Alabama rolled the dice. Punter Bryne Diehl delivered a pass to Tommy Johnson, a cornerback spread wide on the coverage team.

Johnson took the pass completely unattended, cut across field at the Southern Miss 40 to pick up a couple of blocks and went all the way.
Michael Proctor's extra point made it 7-0 after only three minutes and 42 seconds.

......It looked like Bama was on the way to something impressive. Not so.

Southern Miss tied the game on Hamilton's interception return, then took a 10-7 lead when Lance Nations kicked a 33-yard field goal after the fumble recovery.

Alabama's special teams recovered Perry Carter's fumbled punt at the Southern Miss 20. Michael Proctor kicked a 25-yard field goal to tie it 10-10 with :38 left in the third quarter.

The tide offense drew a deep breath and marched 63 yards in 10 plays for the winning touchdown with 10:19 left in the game.

It was all on the ground except for one 17 yard completion from Jay Barker to Curtis Brown. Chris Anderson had a 16-yard run but the rest was nickel and dime stuff.

The Tide got a break when pass interference on Southern Miss in the end zone moved it to the 2-yard line with a first down. Anderson scored on a 1-yard run. Proctor kicked the final point.

It appeared the only way Southern Mississippi was going to score was a fluke play, and the Bama defense wasn't giving any of them away.

Southern Mississippi's defense wasn't the equal of Alabama's, but it was tough. The Tide had 183 yards rushing and 200 passing, 73 by the punter.

Anderson was Alabama's leader with 67 yards from 15 carries. Derrick Lassic had 28 yards on 7 carries, but did not play after fumbling at the Bama 20 early in the third quarter.

Barker was 13-of-21 for 127 yards with one interception.

Southern Miss' leading rusher was Dwayne Nel-

TOP 25 AP POLL
1. MIAMI
2. WASHINGTON
3. FLORIDA STATE
4. FLORIDA
5. TEXAS A&M
6. MICHIGAN
7. NOTRE DAME
8. SYRACUSE
9. **ALABAMA**
10. PENN STATE
11. COLORADO
12. NEBRASKA
13. OKLAHOMA
14. TENNESSEE
15. UCLE
16. NORTH CAROLINA STATE
17. CLEMSON
18. STANFORD
19. GEORGIA
20. VIRGINIA
21. OHIO STATE
22. GEORGIA TECH
23. SAN DIEGO STATE
24. MISSISSIPPI STATE
25. MISSISSIPPI

son with 28 yards on 9 carries. Quarterback Tommy Waters competed only 7-of-9 passes for 26 yards, was intercepted once and sacked five times.

More changes; walking wounded, and a passel of trouble for Palmer

Michael Rogers started at inside linebacker against Southern Mississippi after backing up Mario Morris against Vandy. The backup role apparently was a message from Stallings to Rogers, who had been inconsistent in fall scrimmages.

Quarterback Barker was limping during the week after twisting an ankle. The situation was so bad that Stallings did not want to include the sophomore in practice.

Sophomore star David Palmer found himself in deep trouble after a second drinking-and-driving arrest the week before the Southern Mississippi game.

There was speculation that Stallings might toss him off the team. Instead the coach pulled him from the playing field indefinitely. It was an issue that disrupted Stallings' and the team's flow.

GAME STATS AND SCORING

Alabama	7	0	3	7	17
Southern Miss	0	0	10	0	10

STATISTICS	UA	USM
First Downs	19	3
Rushing (Atts/Yds)	51-183	27-28
Passing (Comp/Atts/Int)	14-22-1	7-19-1
Passing Yards	200	26
Total Offense	383	54
Average Gain Per Play	5.25	1.18
Fumbles/Lost	6-2	1-1
Total Turnovers	3	2
Punting(No/Avg)	6-37.5	11-43.1
Punt Returns(No/Yds)	7-23	4-4
Kickoff Returns(No/Yds)	2-35	3-82
Penalties/Yards	9-78	10-81
Time of Possession	36:13	23:47
Third Down Conversions	1-12	1-14
Fourth Down Conversions	1-1	0-0
Sacks/Lost	5-24	1-6

INDIVIDUAL STATISTICS

Rushing (Att-Yds-TD): UA-Lassic 7-28-0; S. Williams 8-28-0; Houston 8-22-0; Anderson 15-67-1; Wimbley 1-7-0; Lynch 4-18-0; Barker 8-13-0. USM-Waters 7-(-27)-0; Welch 9-10-0; Nelson 8-28-1; Buckhalter 1-2-0; R. Jones 1-13-0; McKinney 1-2-0.

Passing(Comp-Att-I-Yds-TD): UA-Barker 13-21-1-127-0; Diehl 1-1-0-73-1. USM-Waters 7-19-1-26-0.

Receiving(Rec-Yds-TD): UA-Wimbley 2-25-0; Lassic 5-38-0; Tom. Johnson 1-73-1; C. Brown 1-17-0; Busky 1-16-0; Lee 1-9-0; S. Williams 1-6-0; Anderson 2-16-0. USM-McKinney 2-1-0; Welch 3-6-0; Pope 1-14-0; Montgomery 1-5-0.

DEFENSIVE STATISTICS

Tackles (Primary-Assists-Total): UA—Hall 5-3-8; Copeland 4-1-5; London 5-2-7; Curry 5-1-6; Tom. Johnson 2-2-4. USM—Nix 7-5-12; Rankins 6-3-9; Tobias 6-3-9; Harmon 5-3-8.

Sacks: UA—Curry 4 (-12); Hall 1 (-5); Copeland 1 (-7). USM-Singleton 1 (-6).

Tackles for Losses: UA—Hall 2 (-6); Curry 1 (-5); Gregory 1 (-3). USM—Hamilton 1 (-8); Harmon 1 (-4).

Passes Broken Up: UA—Teague 2; Donnelly 1. USM-Rankins 1.

Interceptions: UA—Langham 1. USM-Hamilton 1.

Fumbles Recovered: UA—Tom.Johnson 1. USM-Ratcliff 1.

Fumbles Caused: UA—Tom. Johnson 1. USM-Robinson 1.

Quarterback Pressures: UA—Curry 4; Copeland, Nunley (2 each); London, Hall (1 each). USM—none.

SCORING SUMMARY

First Quarter
UA 7, USM 0—11:18 Tommy Johnson 73-yard pass from Bryne Diehl (Michael Proctor kick) [4 plays, 75 yards, 1:42]

Third Quarter
UA 7, USM 7—13:52 Bobby Hamilton 18-yard int. return (Lance Nations kick)
UA 7, USM 10—11:29 Nations 33-yard field goal [4 plays, 3 yards, 1:48]
UA 10, USM 10—:31 Proctor 25-yard field goal [9 plays, 64 yards, 4:19]

Fourth Quarter
UA 17, USM 10—10:19 Chris Anderson 1-yard run (Proctor kick) [10 plays, 63 yards, 4:01]

Stallings' decision is proper one

By Clyde Bolton

The David Palmer situation reminds me of a cartoon I saw in a magazine.

The warden of a penitentiary was standing at the front gate with an inmate who had served his sentence. The thief was assuring the warden he'd learned his lesson and would never return to the slammer—and all the while he was picking the warden's pocket.

As punishment for a drunk driving episode, Alabama coach Gene Stallings held Palmer out of the opening game of the season Saturday.

Palmer's response was to go out after the game and get himself arrested on another charge of driving under the influence of alcohol.

If he is guilty, Palmer should be ashamed of himself, for he betrayed Stallings, the staff, his teammates, the fans, the Alabama tradition. He should apologize and mean it.

But, when all is said and done, Stallings made the proper decision in not severing the lifeline between the university and Palmer.

Another chance

Palmer got a chance to redeem himself and blew it, and now he is getting another chance. That is merciful on Stallings' part, but it isn't excessively merciful.

Stallings said simply that the sophomore from Birmingham has been suspended indefinitely. "That may be three weeks and it may be three months." Of course, it could be forever.

Palmer will continue to live in the dormitory, continue to attend class, continue to practice. Clearly, the ball is in his court—or, considering the season, perhaps we should say on his side of the 50.

I hope David Palmer is man enough to be grateful for his new chance and make the most of it. I hope he doesn't blow an Alabama and/or professional football career and end up wearing overalls and pushing a wide broom down a hall and thinking about what might have been.

"I think in David's situation now he needs us, he needs me," Stallings said. "I'm not going to turn my back on him."

Gene Stallings is a good man. Most people don't know how good, for he won't advertise it. "Now, this is off the record," he's always insisting when he fears he may be about to tell me a story that is too revealing of his nature. I know some things about Gene Stallings that would amaze you.

Not only did Stallings do the right thing, college football did the right thing. The sport has used kids for a long time—unpaid coolies whose labor has enriched coaches and enabled schools to build magnificent buildings. But this time college football didn't execute one of its own.

Easy way out

And be sure that the easy way out for Stallings would have been to kick Palmer off the squad. "Boy hidy, Gene's as touch as ole Bear, ain't he?" fans would say, forgetting that in his later years ole Bear gave some kids multiple chances to get it right.

Booting Palmer would have served no purpose. It could have destroyed the chances of a poor kid to live an improved life. Keeping him won't infect the team. It probably will give the players even more respect for their coach.

Of course, some folks will scoff that Stallings is merely according star treatment to a star, hoping he will straighten himself out and help Alabama win football games in the future. I don't believe that.

Is Palmer dependent on alcohol? "I don't know," Stallings said. "I wish I could answer that for you...I know his judgment hasn't been very good."

If he is, he should be helped, and I'm convinced he will be. If he isn't—if he's just a 19-year-old kid acting world-class stupid—he should start behaving like a real man.

A good role model would be Gene Stallings.

Derrick Lassic takes a tumble against Arkansas defenders here, but overall it was a day for the offense.

Some Offense Shows Up
Arkansas

Bama finds offense, routs Razorbacks

By Jimmy Bryan

LITTLE ROCK, ARK., Sept. 20—Two surprise guests made grand entrances after the Alabama-Arkansas football game began in War Memorial Stadium here Saturday night: Arkansas governor and front-running presidential candidate Bill Clinton and the Alabama offense.

Clinton was advertised to show up, but didn't arrive until 11 minutes remained in the first quarter. The Alabama offense was a mystery guest.

Nobody knew if it would show up or not.

But for the first time this season, the offense joined hands with the Crimson Steel Curtain defense and the finished product was a dominating 38-11 victory before a stadium-record crowd of 55,912.

Alabama quarterback Jay Barker passed for three touchdowns before retiring late in the third quarter. Derrick Lassic rushed for 118 yards on 18 carries.

Five different players scored touchdowns for the Tide as it rolled up 467 yards offense.

The defense was it usual dominating self, giving up only one touchdown late and 196 yards offense. It was a mercy killing by the Tide, which took a 28-0 half-time lead and pulled back on the throttle in the second half. It improved Alabama's record to 3-0 overall and 2-0 in the SEC. Arkansas dropped 1-2,1-1.

Cussed and discussed after producing only five touchdowns in the last six regular-season games dating back to last year-two TDs in struggling performances against Vanderbilt and Southern Mississippi this season-the Tide offense exploded early against the Razorbacks.

Tailback Lassic ignited it with a 33-yard touchdown run of Alabama's first play from scrimmage. Arkansas had the ball first but went back 10 yards.

The Crimson Tide offense battered Arkansas with a 99-yard drive in 15 plays late in the opening quarter.

Alabama didn't stop there. The Tide drove 89 yards in eight plays in the second quarter and the game was essentially over at 21-0.

Then, to show it hadn't lost its touch, the defense set up one more first-half touchdown when Sam Shade intercepted a pass at the Razorbacks' 24. The offense cashed this one in six plays and it was 28-0 at the half. After Lassic jolted Arkansas with his lightning bolt, Barker and the offense punished the Razorbacks with a beauty of a drive.

Backed to its own 1-yard line after Antonio Langham's pass interception, the Tide came off its goal line. Lassic's 14-yard run on third-and-six was the play that jump-started it.

Barker passed 19 yards to Dabo Sweeney, 8 yards to Kevin Lee and Chris Anderson ran 15 yards in the big plays that reached the Arkansas 23. Alabama went on to the 13, but a holding penalty shoved in back to the 22.

On third-and-19 from the Arkansas 22, Barker delivered a shovel pass to Anderson, who fled to the end zone. Michael Proctor kicked his second extra

TOP 25 AP POLL
1. MIAMI
2. WASHINGTON
3. FLORIDA STATE
4. MICHIGAN
5. TEXAS A&M
6. NOTRE DAME
7. **ALABAMA**
8. TENNESSEE
9. PENN STATE
10. COLORADO
11. UCLA
12. OHIO STATE
13. FLORIDA
14. VIRGINIA
15. NEBRASKA
16. CLEMSON
17. SYRACUSE
18. GEORGIA
19. STANFORD
20. OKLAHOMA
21. SAN DIEGO STATE
22. SOUTHERN CAL
23. NORTH CAROLINA STATE
24. KANSAS
25. BOSTON COLLEGE

point and it was 14-0 after the first quarter.

The Tide got Proctor in position to attempt a 48-yard field goal two plays into the second quarter, but it was short.

The next time Alabama got it, the offense didn't come up short. It pieced together another beauty of 89 yards. Lassic had a 21-yard run, followed by a 19-yard reverse by Lee and then a 36-yard Barker to Anderson pass to the Arkansas 5.

Barker passed to tight end Steve Buskey on third-and-two for the touchdown. Proctor kicked it to 21-0.

Alabama drove to Arkansas 25, but Barker fumbled on third down and Arkansas recovered. However, Shade intercepted Jason Allen on the next play at the Razorback 25 and the Tide cashed it.

Barker passed to Lee for a 5-yard touchdown on third down. Proctor's kick made it 28-0 at the half.

Arkansas had three first downs, 2 net yards rushing and 29 yards passing at the half. Alabama had 15 first downs, 175 yards rushing and 124 yards passing. That's how dominating the Tide was.

Alabama pulled back on the throttle after intermission.

Each team had a field goal in the third quarter. Arkansas got its three points first, on Todd Wright's 27-yarder with 5:48 left.

Alabama matched it on Proctor's 22-yarder with 1:20. It was 31-3 turning to the fourth quarter.

The Tide's George Teague blocked an Arkansas punt at midfield on the final play of the third quarter. Alabama stepped off a 50-yard drive in 10 plays. By this stage, Brian Burgdorf had replaced Barker at quarterback. Barker suffered a minor ankle twist and could have returned, but this one was in the bank. Sherman Williams starred in Burgdorf's first touchdown drive as an Alabama quarterback. He reeled off a 23-yard run to the Arkansas 1-yard line, and two plays later scored from there. Proctor's kick made it 38-3.

The Razorbacks got a window-dressing touchdown late in the game. A 15-yard penalty against the Tide on a punting down for 12-men on the field gave

Arkansas new life.

Barry Lunney passed to Ron Dickerson for a 6-yard touchdown with 1:02 left. The same combination produced a 2-point conversion to arrive at he final score.

Arkansas got an onside kick and drove back to the Alabama 10, but the game ended there.

Hogs give 3-0 Tide high praise

Before Arkansas quarterback Jason Allen was replaced by freshman Barry Lunney late in Saturday night's game at Little Rock, he experienced the sound and the fury of Alabama's heralded defensive unit.

As the Crimson Tide was pounding the Razor-backs 38-11 for its 13th straight win, Allen was taking a beating from nose tackle James Gregory and ends Eric Curry, John Copeland and Jeremy Nunley.
Allen thought he had played against the quickest, fastest, most physical defensive front there was in the college ranks when national champion Miami came to Little Rock last season and came away with a 31-3 victory.

"I didn't think I would see that kind of talent again," said Allen. "I knew Alabama had a great defense, especially up front, but they're much quicker than any of us expected. You don't see too many college linemen as big as they are who are that quick."

Critical injury

Defensive star Eric Curry fractured his left hand against Arkansas and underwent minor surgery Sunday night, Sept. 20.

However, Coach Stallings said he was optimistic Curry might play against Louisiana Tech on Saturday. "It's just a small fracture," he said, "if there is such a thing."

GAME STATS AND SCORING

Alabama	14	14	3	7	38
Arkansas	0	0	3	8	11

STATISTICS	UA	AR
First Downs	24	13
Rushing (Atts/Yds)	51-240	25-28
Passing (Comp/Atts/Int)	18-26-1	17-35-3
Passing Yards	227	164
Total Offense	467	192
Average Gain Per Play	5.8	5.9
Fumbles/Lost	5-3	3-3
Total Turnovers	4	6
Punting(No/Avg)	2-35.5	6-36.5
Punt Returns(No/Yds)	2-23	4-38
Kickoff Returns(No/Yds)	2-3	4-104
Penalties/Yards	8-95	4-20
Time of Possession	35:56	24:04
Third Down Conversions	9-15	1-12
Fourth Down Conversions	0-0	1-1
Sacks/Lost	3-17	2-15

INDIVIDUAL STATISTICS

Rushing (Att-Yds-TD): UA-Lassic 18-112-1; Williams 9-32-1; Houston 7-23-0; Anderson 3-15-0; Lee 1-19-0; Lynch 2-6-0; Harris 1-4-0; Barker 7-9-0. AR-Jackson 8-20-0; Jeffery 6-17-0; Lunney 3-5-0; Pryor 2-4-0; Preston 1-(-1)-0; Allen 5-(-17)-0.

Passing(Comp-Att-I-Yds-TD): UA-Barker 14-17-0-192-3; Burgdorf 4-9-1-35-0 AR-Lunney 9-14-0-96-1; Allen 7-20-3-63-0; Preston 1-1-0-5-0.

Receiving(Rec-Yds-TD): UA-Anderson 4-69-1; Wimbley 2-27-0; C. Brown 3-64; Swinney 1-19-0; Lee 2-13-1; Busky 1-2-1; Houston 3-16-0; Williams 1-9-0; Lassic 1-8-0.
AR-Pryor 2-56-0; Botkin 5-41-0; Dickerson 4-37-1; Caldwell 3-22-0; Jeffery 1-6-0; Jackson 1-1-0; Lunney 1-1-0.

DEFENSIVE STATISTICS

Tackles (Primary-Assists-Total): UA—Hall 4-3-7; Rogers 3-3-6; Teague 2-2-4.
AR—Chatman 4-5-9; Kempf 1-7-8.
Sacks: UA—Jefferies 2 (-12); Nunley 1 (-5).
AR—Long 1 (-7); Kelly 1 (-8).
Tackles for Losses: UA—Jefferies 2 (-12); Nunley 1 (-5); Rogers 2 (-3).
AR—Kelly 3 (-16); Long 2 (-8); Ford 1 (-9); Soli 1 (-2).
Passes Broken Up: UA—Morris, Copeland (1 each).
AR—Ireland, Jackson (1 each).
Interceptions: UA—Shade 2, Langham 1. AR-Kennedy 1.
Fumbles Recovered: UA—Royal, Curry, Jefferies (1 each).
AR—Nunnerley, Long (1 each).
Fumbles Caused: UA—Teague 1. AR-Chatman 1.
Blocked kicks: UA—Teague 1.
Quarterback Pressures: UA—Curry 7; London, Copeland (3 each); Hall 2; Nunley 1.

SCORING SUMMARY

First Quarter
UA 7, AR 0—12:40 Derrick Lassic 33-yard run (Michael Proctor PAT) [1 play, 33 yards, :09]
UA 14, AR 0—7:03 Chris Anderson 22-yard pass from Jay Barker (Proctor PAT) [15 plays, 99 yards, 7:40]
Second Quarter
UA 21, AR 0—9:10 Steve Busky 2-yard pass from Barker (Proctor PAT) [8 plays, 89 yards, 3:05]
UA 28, AR 0—:33 Kevin Lee 5-yard pass from Barker (Proctor PAT) [6 plays, 24 yards, 3:01]
Third Quarter
UA 28, AR 3—5:48 Todd Wright 27-yard field goal [11 plays, 44 yards, 5:30]
UA 31, AR 3—1:28 Proctor 22-yard field goal [9 plays, 60 yards, 4:20]
Fourth Quarter
UA 38, AR 3—11:05 Sherman Williams 1-yard run [10 plays, 50 yards, 3:55]
UA 38, AR 11—1:02 Ron Dickerson 6-yard pass from Barry Lunney (Conversion to Dickerson from Lunney) [12 plays, 82 yards, 4:39]

La. Tech defense—called toughest of the year by Jay Barker—closes in on the Alabama quarterback

Defense Sets the Tone

Louisiana Tech

Deuce, defense lift Tide

By Jimmy Bryan

The Deuce got loose one time at Legion Field Saturday, and that was all the cushion Alabama's defense needed to do its normal intimidating thing against Louisiana Tech.

David Palmer, The Deuce, made his first appearance after sitting out a three-game suspension for two DUI violations. He returned a punt 63 yards with 8:18 left in the game to put the cushion in place for a 13-0 Alabama win before 77,622.

Palmer and the Crimson Tide's mighty defense, ranked No. 1 in the nation, rescued an Alabama offense that again lost its way. The offense failed to put a touchdown in Louisiana Tech's end zone, after piling five in against Arkansas last week.

Louisiana Tech's touch defense had something to do with that, however. The Bulldogs almost matched the Tide defense hit for hit.

Alabama's defense pounded Tech for minus-8 rushing, 125 passing and strapped the Bulldogs with their first shutout in 45 games. Louisiana Tech stuck the Tide with 67 net yards rushing and an even 100 passing. This was no offensive explosion.

Alabama quarterback Jay Barker completed only 11 of 23 passes for 100 yards, was intercepted once and sacked five times. Martin Houston was the leading rusher with a career-best 73 yards from 19 carries. Tech starting quarterback Sam Hughes completed 8 of 19 for 113 yards and was sacked three times before leaving the game just over seven minutes left in the third quarter. Back-up Aaron Ferguson was 5 of 7 for 12 yards and was sacked twice going the rest of the way.

The Bulldogs' leading rusher was Jason Cooper with 21 yards from 11 carries.

Alabama did enough to run its record to 4-0 and at least protect its No. 7 national ranking. Louisiana Tech came even at 2-2.

Alabama was hanging to a shaky, and vulnerable, lead of 6-0 from a pair of Michael Proctor field goals going into the fourth quarter.

Then, backed to his 14-yard line, Tech punter Daryl Altic unloaded a 49-yarder that was a little more than his coverage could handle. Palmer caught it at the Bama 37, quickly dodged the first potential tackler and got behind a wall of blockers.

Finally, only Altic stood between Palmer and the end zone—and this was a bad mismatch. Palmer ran easily past the kicker to put the game away. Proctor's extra point made it 13-0 and 8:18 remained. But Louisiana Tech wasn't up to scoring against Alabama's defense.

"I thought the best thing about the game was both sides played really outstanding defense," Tide coach Gene Stallings said. "I thought their defense played really well. We played well also, especially when they had the ball down on our goal line (four shots from the Bama 4-yard-line in the third quarter, Bama up 6-0).

"We were having a hard time holding onto the ball. We missed several passes. The running game never got in sync. I was disappointed in the running game. We didn't protect the quarterback very well and they trapped him several times."

TOP 25 AP POLL
1. WASHINGTON
2. MIAMI
3. FLORIDA STATE
4. MICHIGAN
5. TEXAS A&M
6. NOTRE DAME
7. TENNESSEE
8. PENN STATE
9. **ALABAMA**
10. COLORADO
11. UCLA
12. OHIO STATE
13. FLORIDA
14. VIRGINIA
15. NEBRASKA
16. GEORGIA
17. SYRACUSE
18. STANFORD
19. OKLAHOMA
20. SOUTHERN CAL
21. NORTH CAROLINA STATE
22. BOSTON COLLEGE
23. GEORGIA TECH
24. MISSISSIPPI STATE
25. CLEMSON

"The kicking game helped in some areas. We kicked two-for-two field goals and returned a punt. They missed a field goal."

Louisiana Tech coach Joe Raymond Peace saw the same game Stallings saw.

"There were two great defenses out there playing," he said. "I said going in I had never been so impressed with a defense as Alabama's. After playing them, I feel the same.

"We had our chances. We had first-and-four to go ahead, or at least get a field goal. If we get some points, it could change the complexion of the game. We just couldn't do it. We didn't execute offensively all day."

As it had done all year, the Alabama defense sent the other team backward on the first series. Louisiana Tech was a yard worse off on fourth down than when it started.

Tech's defense outdid Alabama on its first crack at the Tide. Alabama started from its 24, and wound up at its 10 on fourth down.

The ground rules were pretty much established, although Alabama's offense made its most impressive move on the next series. Starting at its 22, Bama drove to the Tech 19 in 11 plays but stalled there.

Proctor kicked a 37-yard field goal with 4:48 to go in the first quarter to stake Bama to a 3-0 lead that would actually be good enough.

The Tide started its next drive from the Tech 30 after a 15-yard penalty against the Bulldogs for interfering with Palmer's right to a fair catch. Bama got a first down at the 15, but nothing more as the first quarter ended.

Proctor kicked a 35-yard field goal on the first play of the second quarter and it was 6-0.

The Bulldogs got to the Alabama 40 late in the second quarter, but the Tide pushed them back to midfield. Alabama made no serious moves after Proctor's second field goal.

Tech had its one solid opportunity at the Alabama goal line on its first offensive thrust of the third quarter.

Looking at third-and-11 at his 29, quarterback Hughes and wide receiver John Henry hooked up on a

61-yard pass play to the Alabama 9-yard-line. The Tide was caught offside on first down, so it became first-and-goal from the 4.

The Tide defense put the pressure on and Louisiana Tech went like this: no gain, incomplete pass, incomplete pass. Chris BONIOL had a 22-yard chip shot field goal, but jerked it left and the Tide kept its shutout.

There would be no serious scoring opportunities for Louisiana Tech after that. The Tide defense had been awakened to the fact that one fluke play could mean the game. It allowed none.

Tech never came on Alabama's side of the 50-yard line after that.

David Palmer returns from suspension and returns this punt for a touchdown to secure the Alabama victory

GAME STATS AND SCORING

Alabama	3	3	0	7	13
Louisiana Tech	0	0	0	0	0

STATISTICS	UA	TECH
First Downs	14	5
Rushing (Atts/Yds)	44-67	27-(-8)
Passing (Comp/Atts/Int)	11-23-1	13-26-0
Passing Yards	100	125
Total Offense	167	117
Average Gain Per Play	2.49	0.79
Fumbles/Lost	0-0	4-1
Total Turnovers	1	1
Punting(No/Avg)	9-37.0	12-41.8
Punt Returns(No/Yds)	6-80	3-17
Kickoff Returns(No/Yds)	0-0	4-99
Penalties/Yards	5-45	10-101
Time of Possession	32:38	27:22
Third Down Conversions	4-15	1-16
Fourth Down Conversions	0-0	0-0
Sacks/Lost	5-29	5-46

INDIVIDUAL STATISTICS

Rushing (Att-Yds-TD): UA—Lassic 8-23-0; Houston 19-73-0; Anderson 5-7-0; Wimbley 1-9-0; Palmer 2-(-2)-0 Barker 9-(-43)-0.
LT—Cooper 11-21-0; Davis 10-7-0; Hughes 3-(-18)-0; Ferguson 3-(-18)-0.

Passing(Comp-Att-I-Yds-TD): UA—Barker 11-23-1-100-0.
LT—Hughes 8-19-0-113-0; Ferguson 5-7-0-12-0.

Receiving(Rec-Yds-TD): UA—C. Brown 2-28; Palmer 3-22-0; Lee 2-18-0; Wimbley 1-14-0; Lynch 1-3-0; Busky 1-9-0; Houston 1-6-0.
LT—Parham 4-28-0; Kennedy 1-12-0; Davis 2-5-0; Francis 2-16-0; Henry 1-62-0; Thomas 1-8-0; Cooper 2-(-6)-0.

DEFENSIVE STATISTICS

Tackles (Primary-Assists-Total):
UA—Rogers 6-3-9; London 5-2-7; Copeland 4-2-6; Hall 4-2-6.
LT—Cornelius 7-2-9; Piete 5-4-9; Wilson 7-1-8; Baker 5-2-7.

Sacks: UA—London 1 (-9); Langham 1 (-6); Copeland 1 (-3).
LT—Wilson 2 (-14); Evans 1 (-14); Broudy 1 (-13); Cornelius 1 (-5).

Tackles for Losses: UA—Copeland 2 (-6); Nunley 2 (-7); Rogers 1 (-4); London 1 (-1); Hall 1 (-1).
LT—Piete 1 (-7); Baker 1 (-2); Evans 1 (-1).

Passes Broken Up: UA—Hall, Copeland, Gaston, Turner, Shade (1 each).
LT—Broudy 2; Evans, Bolton (1 each).

Interceptions: UA—none.
LT—Prince 1.

Fumbles Recovered: UA—Copeland 1. LT-none.

Fumbles Caused: UA—Copeland 1. LT-none.

Quarterback Pressures: UA—Hall 2; Tom. Johnson, London, Copeland, Gregory (1 each).
LT—Baker 1.

SCORING SUMMARY

First Quarter
UA 3, LT 0—Michael Proctor 37-yard field goal [12 plays, 59 yards, 5:14]

Second Quarter
UA 6, LT 0—Proctor 35-yard field goal [7 plays, 13 yards, 3:30]

Fourth Quarter
UA 13, LT 0—11:05 David Palmer 63-yard punt return (Proctor PAT)

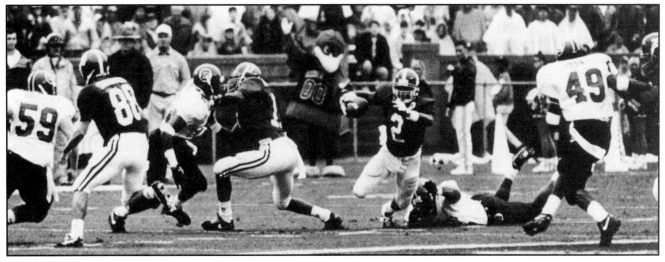

Good line blocking springs Palmer for a gain against Arkansas

Offense Has Its Best Day

South Carolina

Alabama hangs Carolina out to dry; Tide cruises on rainy homecoming

By Jimmy Bryan

TUSCALOOSA, Oct. 4—Alabama spent the first half of a damp, dreary day making the South Carolina Gamecocks' first trip to Bryant-Denny Stadium as miserable as the weather, and spent the second half trying not to humiliate them.

Ninth-ranked Alabama (5-0 overall, 3-0 in the Southeastern Conference) stomped South Carolina (0-5, 0-4) 48-7 to send a sold-out homecoming crowd of 70,123 home singing in the rain. It was Alabama's 15th straight victory, and South Carolina's ninth straight loss.

The beating could have been much more severe. The Crimson Tide led 38-0 at half-time and appeared entirely capable of doubling that in the second half.

But coach Gene Stallings elected to put the speeding Tide on cruise control. He took starting quarter-back Jay Barker out of the game after the first series of the second quarter and never sent him back in.

Stallings went three-deep at quarterback, turning it over to Brian Burgdorf for the second and third quarters and Chad Key in the fourth. He also sent every player dressed for the game, other than redshirt candidates, into the one-sided battle.

Alabama scored 21 points in the first quarter and added 17 in the second while the nation's No. 1-ranked defense strangled South Carolina. This game was definitely over at the half.

"Derrick Lassic ran extremely well in the early part of the game when it really counted. I thought all our backs ran well.

"Overall, the first units played well, although they didn't play much."

The Tide had two 100-yard rushers, Chris Anderson gaining 120 yards on 13 carries and Lassic 100 yards, also on 13 carries. Barker was 5 of 11 for 69 yards passing and Burgdorf 6 of 11 for 60.

Alabama flanker/kick returner David Palmer had a so-so day—for him. His all-purpose count was 118 yards—42 from four rushing attempts, 11 receiving from one catch, 44 from four punt returns and 21 from one kickoff return.

South Carolina was stuck with only 43 yards rushing, the Bama D's fourth straight game holding an opponent under 100 yards.

South Carolina coach Sparky Woods should have sent Stallings a thank you note for holding the score down.

Alabama established domination on the game's first series. Back to its 13-yard line after a holding penalty on the opening kickoff, Alabama went 87 yards in a lightning-quick five plays. And that established the ground rules for the day.

After exchanging punts, Palmer ran the next kick 24 yards to the Gamecocks' 33. The Tide went home in three plays, the touchdown a 14-yard run by Sherman Williams.

TOP 25 AP POLL

1. WASHINGTON
2. MIAMI
3. MICHIGAN
4. TENNESSEE
5. TEXAS A&M
6. **ALABAMA**
7. PENN STATE
8. FLORIDA STATE
9. COLORADO
10. VIRGINIA
11. STANFORD
12. GEORGIA
13. NOTRE DAME
14. NEBRASKA
15. SYRACUSE
16. OKLAHOMA
17. GEORGIA TECH
18. MISSISSIPPI STATE
19. UCLA
20. SOUTHERN CAL
21. BOSTON COLLEGE
22. OHIO STATE
23. FLORIDA
24. CALIFORNIA
25. CLEMSON

Two plays after South Carolina got the ball at its 13 on the kickoff, Bama's Bryan Thornton recovered a fumble at the 14. Chris Anderson got the touchdown with runs of 8 and 6 yards.

With Proctor's extra points it was 21-0 at the end of the first quarter.

On its first drive of the second quarter, Barker unleashed the passing game. He hit Palmer for 11, Curtis Brown for 13 and finally Brown for 25 and the touchdown.

The Bama defense threw up its roadblock again and Carolina's Marty Simpson got away only a 27-yard punt from his 11-yard line. The Tide flashed 37 yards in five plays.

Alabama receiver Curtis Brown outruns gamecock defenders for another gain in fine offensive effort

Craig Harris scored on a 5-yard run and it became 35-0.

When Alabama got the ball again, Burgdorf got it positioned for a 31-yard Proctor field goal. It was 38-0.

Freshman Steve Taneyhill led South Carolina on its best drive. It went from the Gamecocks' 25 to the Alabama 13 where it died on fourth-and-six just before the half.

Alabama had far more points than it would need, and Stallings chose not to be greedy.

The only points of the third quarter came from Hamp Greene's 27-yard field goal with 3:21 left in the period.

South Carolina scored late, then Chris Anderson broke a 37-yard run for the final touchdown on a play that was designed to do little more than run the clock out.

Said Anderson, "I always give 100 percent. There was a big hole, and once I got through, it was a foot race. I won."

Steve Taneyhill, who chose SC over BAMA, is given a rough welcome in his first game against the Tide

Still untested? Not for long

Following the South Carolina game, staffer Charles Hollis wrote that while Alabama remains unbeaten, it also remains untested—having yet to face a ranked opponent.

And, "barring a total collapse Saturday night in New Orleans against the Tulane Green Wave (2-2), the Tide should improve" to 6-0.

He reminded readers that the easy road was about to come to an end. For the following week "the Tide travels to Knoxville to face No. 4 Tennessee."

And then, for the first time since spring training, the mention showed up in public again: "A victory over the Volunteers, a team Alabama has beaten the past six seasons, would put the Tide in the middle of the national championship race."

At this point, eight undefeated teams remained: Washington, Miami, Tennessee, Texas A&M, Penn State, Colorado, Virginia and Alabama.

"It's too early to be talking about the national championship," said Stallings. "Sure, it's possible. But lots of things can happen between now and the end of the season. There is still a lot of football to play.

"How you're ranked in the fourth or fifth game is

not what is important. We're (ranked sixth), whatever that means. Texas A&M barely beat (Texas Tech 17-16) and moved up. You can't tell what's going to happen. We still have the toughest part of our schedule to go."

GAME STATS AND SCORING

| Alabama | 21 | 17 | 3 | 7 | 48 |
| South Carolina | 0 | 0 | 0 | 7 | 7 |

STATISTICS	UA	USC
First Downs	29	9
Rushing (Atts/Yds)	54-356	37-43
Passing (Comp/Atts/Int)	11-22-1	11-24-0
Passing Yards	129	148
Total Offense	485	191
Average Gain Per Play	6.38	3.13
Fumbles/Lost	2-1	7-2
Total Turnovers	2	2
Punting(No/Avg)	4-35.0	10-37.6
Punt Returns(No/Yds)	5-44	1-2
Kickoff Returns(No/Yds)	2-41	8-170
Penalties/Yards	5-36	6-36
Time of Possession	32:49	27:11
Third Down Conversions	6-13	4-15
Fourth Down Conversions	0-0	1-3
Sacks/Lost	4-33	2-5

INDIVIDUAL STATISTICS

Rushing (Att-Yds-TD): UA—Anderson 13-120-2; Lassic 13-100-1; Palmer 4-42-0; Williams 7-33-1; Houston 6-35-0; Harris 3-16-1; Lynch 4-12-0; Burgdorf 7-2-0; Key 1-(-4)-0.
USC—Bennett 8-26-1; Wilburn 8-20-0; Reddick 3-19-0; Henry 2-0-0; Williamson 2-(-17)-0; Tanneyhill 6-(-10)-0.
Passing(Comp-Att-I-Yds-TD): UA—Barker 5-11-1-69-1; Burgdorf 6-11-0-60-0.
USC—Tanneyhill 10-17-0-135-0; Williamson 1-17-0-13-0.
Receiving(Rec-Yds-TD): UA—Wimbley 2-9-0; C. Brown 3-46-1; Swinney 2-22-0; Lynch 1-11-1; Palmer 1-1-0; Williams 1-15-0.
USC—Penny 2-67-0; Harris 2-19-0; Henry 1-14-0; Cates 1-17-0; Bennett 2-11-0; Chaney 1-9-0; Reddick 1-6-0; Pender 1-5-0.

DEFENSIVE STATISTICS

Tackles (Primary-Assists-Total): UA—Lockett 5-0-5; W. Brown 4-1-5; Morris 4-1-5.
USC—Watkins 5-4-9; Greene 3-5-8; Smith 3-5-8.
Sacks: UA—Hall 2 (-17); W. Brown 1 (-9); S. Brown 1 (-8).
USC—Reed 1 (-4); Bettiford 1 (-1)
Tackles for Losses: UA—Thornton 1 (-6); S. Brown 1 (-2); W. Brown 1 (-3).
USC—Sullivan 1 (-12); Long 2 (-8); Greene 1 (-6); Bettiford 1 (-5).
Passes Broken Up: UA—Gaston, Oden (1 each).
USC—Franklin, Mitchell (1 each).
Interceptions: UA—none. USC—Adams 1.
Fumbles Recovered: UA-Walters, Thornton (1 each).
USC-Bemberg 1.
Fumbles Caused: UA—Gregory 1. USC—Reed 1.
Quarterback Pressures: UA—W. Brown, Hall, E. Brown, Copeland (1 each).
USC—Watkins, Bettiford (1 each).

SCORING SUMMARY

First Quarter
UA 7, USC 0—13:40 Derrick Lassic 1-yard run (Michael Proctor PAT) [5 plays, 87 yards, 1:20]
UA 14, USC 0—6:40 Sherman Williams 14-yard run (Proctor PAT) [3 plays, 33 yards, 1:10]
UA 21, USC 0—5:25 Chris Anderson 6-yard run (Proctor PAT) [2 plays 14 yards, :44]
Second Quarter
UA 28, USC 0—12:54 Curtis Brown 25-yard pass from Jay Barker (Proctor PAT) [5 plays, 66 yards, 1:16]
UA 35, USC 0—9:05 Craig Harris 5-yard run (Proctor PAT) [5 plays, 37 yards, 1:42]
UA 38, USC 0—2:05 Proctor 31-yard field goal [11 plays, 47 yards, 4:39
Third Quarter
UA 41, USC 0—3:21 Hamp Greene 24-yard field goal [7 plays, 34 yards, 2:52]
Fourth Quarter
UA 41, USC 7—14:36 Brandon Bennett 1-yard run (Marty Simpson PAT) [7 plays, 32 yards, 3:45]
UA 48, USC 7—:52 Anderson 37-yard run (Greene PAT) [4 plays, 61 yards, 1:51]

Barker passed for only 73 yards against Green Wave, but running game blew out Tulane

Confidence Builder for Tennessee

Tulane

Alabama streaks past Green Wave

By Jimmy Bryan

NEW ORLEANS, Oct. 11—Alabama's offense took another step backward in the first half against Tulane

Saturday night, then took some mighty leaps forward in the second.

Held to two field goals in the first half," coach Gene Stallings said. "I was really pleased with the second half effort of the football team. We came out in the second half and did the things we had to do to get the kind of win we needed.

"All the backs ran hard. I thought they gave an outstanding effort."

A superdome crowd of 50,240 saw senior tailback Derrick Lassic explode for 188 yards on 20 carries, and finally open the door to Tulane's end zone with the Tide's first touchdown in the third quarter.

After that, Chris Anderson knocked in two touchdowns and Sherman Williams another to send some 20,000 Alabama fans happily toward Bourbon Street. Anderson broke a long one for the second straight week, wheeling 57 yards with 1:07 left.

Michael Proctor kicked three field goals in four attempts.

The Tide's second-half explosion

TOP 25 AP POLL
1. WASHINGTON
2. MIAMI
3. MICHIGAN
4. **ALABAMA**
5. TEXAS A&M
6. FLORIDA STATE
7. COLORADO
8. STANFORD
9. PENN STATE
10. GEORGIA
11. NEBRASKA
12. NOTRE DAME
13. TENNESSEE
14. SYRACUSE
15. MISSISSIPPI STATE
16. GEORGIA TECH
17. VIRGINIA
18. SOUTHERN CAL
19. CLEMSON
20. BOSTON COLLEGE
21. NORTH CAROLINA STATE
22. WASHINGTON STATE
23. FLORIDA
24. WEST VIRGINIA
25. KANSAS

led to a season-high 435 yards on the ground. Behind Lassic, Anderson rushed for 84 yards on just 7 carries, Martin Houston bulled for 65 on 9, Williams added 48 from only 5 opportunities and David Palmer brought back 42 on three runs. Quarterback Jay Barker didn't have anything eye-catching, 6-for-16 for 73 yards. Brian Burgdorf hit 2-of-3 for 65 yards closing up shop.

The nation-leading defense gave only 58 net yards rushing, but bent for 138 through the air. Still, the secondary stole a season-high four interceptions. The shutout was the second in the last three games.

Derrick Oden and fellow defensemen held Tulane to only 58 yards rushing

Tulane got to the Alabama 49 with the opening kickoff. On fourth-and-1 coach Buddy Teevens elected to punt, to boos from the Green Wave fans.

The Tide was pinned to its 10 by the punt, and despite a 33-yard run by Lassic could get no closer than the Tulane 40. Bryne Diehl punted over the goal. Starting from its 20, Tulane lost back to the 14. On third-and-16, Chip Clark quick-kicked 39 yards to the Alabama 48.

The Crimson Tide took this one to Proctor's first field goal. Lassic broke the first-down play 42 yards to the Tulane 10. The offense went backward from here. Barker lost 6 and was sacked for minus-9. After an incomplete pass, Proctor kicked a 42-yard field goal.

Alabama led 3-0 with 7:40 left in the first quarter. A 36-yard return of the kickoff got Tulane good field position, and a 16-yard personal foul penalty moved it into Alabama territory. The Wave moved to the Tide 34, but Antonio Langham stopped that with an interception at the Tide 15.

Langham's 26-yard return brought it out of danger.

They swapped a punt, and Alabama set out from its 21 only 17 seconds into the second quarter. The Tide pecked away for a couple of first downs, then Barker passed 28 yards to Sherman Williams to the Tulane 28.

Again, the Tide offense couldn't cash it. Proctor missed a 35-yard field goal when the tide declined to go on fourth-and-1 at the Green Wave 19.

The next time Alabama set out from its own 10. Martin Houston broke a 45-yard run on first down. The Tide had little trouble reaching the Tulane 27 with a first down but again didn't find the end zone.

Proctor kicked a 39-yard field goal on fourth-and-5 from the 22. It was 6-0 with 5:06 left in the half.

Tulane almost got a gadget touchdown just before the half. After a 36-yard pass from Shawn Meadows to Wil Ursin got to the Alabama 21, the Green Wave tried a "fumblerooskie" play.

The quarterback left the ball on the ground behind guard Andy Abramowicz, but both his knees were on the ground before he picked up the ball and ran into the end zone. Time ran out before Tulane could kick a field goal.

Alabama started the second half much as it had played the first. Lassic went 27 on one run, the drive reached the Tulane 21, but this was only a momentary setback.

The next time the Tide came into possession, it put one in the end zone. The drive went 57 yards in 9 plays. Lassic had a 17-yard run, and finished it off with a 5-yarder.

Proctor's kick made it 16-0

The next drive went 55 yards in 8 plays, with a Barker-to-Anderson pass getting 20 of it, and Anderson scored from the 2-yard line. Proctor kicked it to 23-0.

Burgdorf took over at quarterback and passed to Tarrant Lynch for 51 yards to the Tulane 4. Williams scored from there and Proctor kicked it to 30-0. Anderson broke his long one to finish it off at 37-0.

GAME STATS AND SCORING

Alabama	3	3	10	21	37
Tulane	0	0	0	0	0

STATISTICS

	UA	TU
First Downs	24	10
Rushing (Atts/Yds)	52-435	32-58
Passing (Comp/Atts/Int)	8-20-0	11-27-4
Passing Yards	138	107
Total Offense	573	165
Average Gain Per Play	8-0	2-8
Fumbles/Lost	2-1	2-0
Total Turnovers	1	4
Punting(No/Avg)	4-43.5	8-41.4
Punt Returns(No/Yds)	3-3-0	2-10-0
Kickoff Returns(No/Yds)	1-32-0	8-174-0
Penalties/Yards	7-68	5-43
Time of Possession	30:18	29:42
Third Down Conversions	9-17	3-14
Fourth Down Conversions	0-0	1-1
Sacks/Lost	2-17	2-13

INDIVIDUAL STATISTICS

Rushing (Att-Yds-TD): UA—Lassic 20-188-1; Anderson 7-84-2; S. Williams 5-48-1; Houston 9-65-0; Palmer 3-42-0; Lynch 2-12-0; Harris 1-2-0; Barker 5-(-6)-0.
TU—Miller 11-26-0; Perry 6-23-0; Hubert 2-8-0; Ducre 3-8-0; Strickland 5-7-0; Abramonowicz 1-0-0; Meadows 4-(-14)-0.

Passing (Comp-Att-I-Yds-TD): UA—Barker 6-16-0-73-0; Burgdorf 2-3-0-65-0; Palmer 1-0-0-0-0.
TU—Meadows 11-26-3-107-0; W. Ursin 1-0-1-0-0.

Receiving (Rec-Yds-TD): UA—Lynch 1-51-0; Williams 1-28-0; Anderson 1-20-0; Palmer 1-14-0; Wimbley 2-10-0; Busky 1-8-0; Swinney 1-7-0.
TU—W. Ursin 3-49-0; J. Ursin 3-35-0; Ballard 1-8-0; Miller 2-7-0; Broadnax 1-6-0; Perry 1-2-0.

DEFENSIVE STATISTICS

Tackles (Primary-Assists-Total): UA—Oden 2-3-5; Gaston 5-0-5; Shade 4-1-5.
TU—Staid 11-0-11; R. Hamilton 8-0-8; Smith 5-1-6.

Sacks: UA—Jeffries 1 (-5); Lockett 1 (-12).
TU—-Batiste 1 (-4); Milano 1 (-9).

Tackles for Losses: UA—Curry 3 (-15); Lockett 1 (-12); Rogers 1 (-1).
TU—Milano 1 (-9); Staid 1 (-5); Batiste 1 (-4); Ducre 1 (-4).

Passes Broken Up: UA—Donnelly, Shade (2 each); Gaston, Langham (1 each).
TU-R. Hamilton 2; McDowell, McGowan (1 each).

Interceptions: UA-Gaston, Donnelly, Langham Teague (1 each).
TU—none.

Fumbles Recovered: UA—none. TU—none.

Fumbles Caused: UA—Oden 1. TU—Staid 2.

Quarterback Pressures: UA—Hall 2; Copeland, Curry, Jeffries, Lockett (1 each).

SCORING SUMMARY

First Quarter
UA 3, TU 0—7:40 Michael Proctor 42-yard field goal [5 plays, 27 yards, 1:57]

Second Quarter
UA 6, TU 0—5:06 Proctor 39-yard field goal [7 plays, 68 yards, 2:54]

Third Quarter
UA 9, TU 0—10:00 Proctor 27-yard field goal [9 plays, 55 yards, 5:00]
UA 16, TU 0—1:26 Derrick Lassic 5-yard run (Proctor PAT) [9 plays, 57 yards, 3:02]

Fourth Quarter
UA 23, TU 0—9:47 Chris Anderson 2-yard run (Proctor PAT) [8 plays, 55 yards, 3:23]
UA 30, TU 0—5:11 Sherman Williams 4-yard run (Proctor PAT) [5 plays, 66 yards, 1:55]
UA 37, TU 0—1:07 Anderson 57-yard run (Proctor PAT) [2 plays, 71 yards, :36]

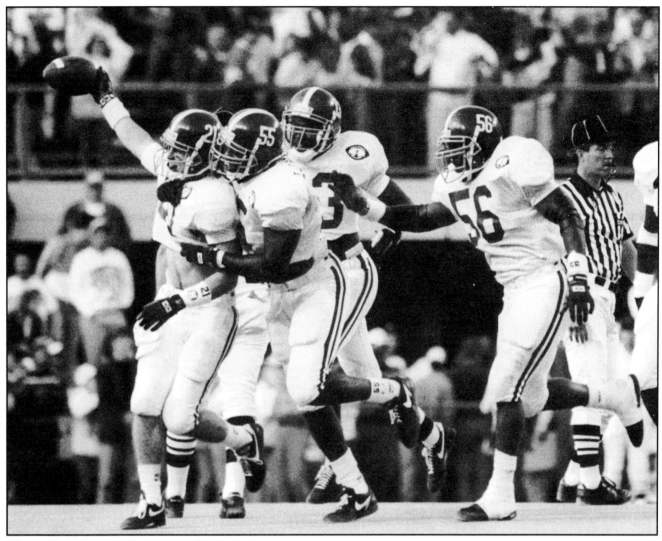

Chris Donnelly steals Tennessee's last hope with a late fourth-quarter interception

Third Saturday in October
...the Tide is Rolling

Tennessee

Bama whips 'em again Tide rolls 7 in Knoxville, all but clinches SEC West

By Jimmy Bryan

KNOXVILLE, Oct. 18—Alabama and Tennessee took another glorious Third Saturday in October to the highest emotional level in Neyland Stadium on Oct. 17, 1992, turning Crimson Tide domination in the first half into the kind of stirring windup this series seems destined to provide year after year.

Alabama held off Tennessee 17-10 during a closing frenzy that left a crowd of 97,388 gasping for oxygen down the stretch.

By strangling the Vols in the clutch, Alabama (7-0 overall, 4-0 SEC) strung together its 17th consecutive victory and took a near death grip on the SEC West championship. Mississippi State's loss to South Carolina provides the Tide with a 2-game lead.

Tennessee dropped to 5-2 overall and 3-2 in the conference to fall a game behind Georgia in the SEC-East.

"That was obviously a big win for us," Tide coach Gene Stallings said. "We played pretty good defense against a pretty good team. Most of the time we were able to

TOP 25 AP POLL
1. MIAMI
2. WASHINGTON
3. MICHIGAN
4. **ALABAMA**
5. TEXAS A&M
6. FLORIDA STATE
7. GEORGIA
8. NEBRASKA
9. COLORADO
10. NOTRE DAME
11. BOSTON COLLEGE
12. SYRACUSE
13. WASHINGTON STATE
14. PENN STATE
15. SOUTHERN CAL
16. STANFORD
17. TENNESSEE
18. CLEMSON
19. GEORGIA TECH
20. FLORIDA
21. ARIZONA
22. KANSAS
23. NORTH CAROLINA STATE
24. VIRGINIA
25. MISSISSIPPI STATE

control the line of scrimmage.

"It was tough out there. We had opportunities to do more, but we did win and that's what's important. We came here and won, so we must be doing something right. It was an outstanding performance by our defense."

Coach Johnny Majors called it one of the most physical games in the storied series.

"I've been involved in a lot of

Derrick Lassick picks up some of his 142 yards in a stellar day against Tennessee. Here fullback Martin Houston throws a key block to spring the runner.

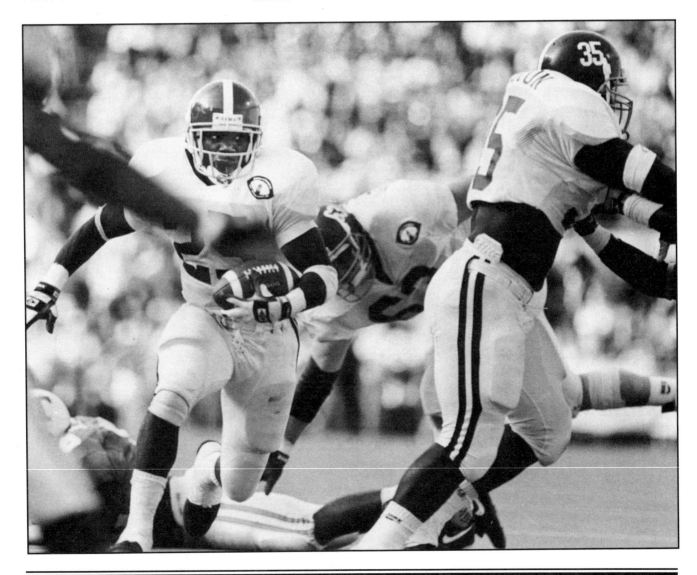

brilliant, hard-fought, tenacious ballgames and many Alabama-Tennessee games," he said. "I don't know when I've seen two teams play with more intensity, effort, mental application and contact in my life.

"You get two teams like this playing so closely there's no guarantee either one will win or lose until the final whistle. I wouldn't do a thing different. I only wish the score was different.

Alabama is a completely solid football team. I don't think there's any question they have grown considerably. They have wonderful talent and made the most of their talent."

Alabama led 17-3 at the half and appeared safely on its way to a comfortable conclusion. It was far from it.

The Crimson Tide failed to score in the second half, once turning down an almost certain field goal on fourth down at the Volunteers' 3-yard line.

Coach Gene Stallings visits with Tennessee coach Johnny Majors who lost his job only weeks after the Alabama loss—a move that Stallings lamented

And when Tennessee stung the proud Alabama defense with a fourth-quarter touchdown, the drama reached stifling proportions.

"I was feeling badly about not going for the field goal down there," Stallings said. "I knew that at the time. But the players had confidence and wanted to go for it.

"It looked like it might come back to haunt us. I made a silly mistake and they bailed me out."

Tennessee had three more opportunities to reach for a tying touchdown after it scored with 12:53 left, but Alabama's mighty defense turned the Vols away impressively.

Tennessee's final gasp came from its 48-yard line when Martin Houston fumbled and Todd Kelly recovered with 1:33 left. Two plays later, safety Chris Donnelly put an end to Volunteer hopes with an intercep-

tion with 1:08 to go.

"We had defensive pressure when we had to have it," Stallings said. "It was a big play by Chris Donnelly."

Alabama controlled this game considerably more than the one-touchdown margin suggests. The Tide held the ball for almost 13 minutes more than Tennessee, rushed for 301 yards and held Tennessee to 78 and piled up 23 first downs to 7.

Tailback Derrick Lassic rushed for 142 yards on 33 carries, his third 100-yard game in a row. He also scored both Alabama touchdowns.

Quarterback Jay Barker completed only 5 of 11 passes for 54 yards, but did not throw an interception. He was sacked three times.

On the other hand, Alabama held Tennessee quarterback Heath Shuler to 12 of 23 for 108 yards, and the only interception was the big one that closed it out. Shuler was sacked five times.

It required three possessions for Alabama to get on the board. Starting from its 46 after winning the field position battle, the Tide drove to a touchdown in eight plays. It was all on the ground.

Lassic shouldered the load with runs of 12, 10 and 16 yards, the last reaching the Tennessee 5-yard line. He knocked it in from the 1-yard line. Michael Proctor's kick made it 7-0 with 5:16 left in the first quarter.

With Charlie Garner ripping off a 44-yard run to the Alabama 33, the Vols got close enough to try a field goal. John Becksvoort missed his first of the season from 42 yards.

Alabama set out from its 25 after the miss, and was driving toward a field goal as the first quarter ended. When the 60-yard march stalled at the UT 15, Proctor kicked a 33-yard field goal to make it 10-0 with 13:42 left in the half.

Tennessee couldn't move the chains with its next possession, and the Tide put together another scoring drive. This went 66 yards in 11 plays, Lassic getting the call eight times. But the big gain was a 33-yard run by Barker to the UT 25. Lassic scored from the 1-yard line and Proctor kicked it to 17-0 with 8:00 left in the half.

GAME STATS AND SCORING

Alabama	7	10	0	0	17
Tennessee	0	3	0	7	10

STATISTICS	UA	UT
First Downs	23	7
Rushing (Atts/Yds)	66-301	26-78
Passing (Comp/Atts/Int)	5-11-0	12-23-1
Passing Yards	54	116
Total Offense	355	194
Average Gain Per Play	4.61	3.96
Fumbles/Lost	4-1	1-0
Total Turnovers	1	1
Punting(No/Avg)	6-39.0	8-38.8
Punt Returns(No/Yds)	4-31	2-47
Kickoff Returns(No/Yds)	2-50	4-183
Penalties/Yards	5-42	3-33
Time of Possession	36:56	23:04
Third Down Conversions	5-14	3-12
Fourth Down Conversions	1-3	1-2
Sacks/Lost	4-21	3-22

INDIVIDUAL STATISTICS

Rushing (Att-Yds-TD): UA—Lassic 33-142-2; Houston 9-57-0; Anderson 7-19-0; Palmer 2-34-0; Lee 1-24-0; Lynch 2-7-0; Williams 2-1-0; Barker 10-17-0.
UT—Garner 7-80-0; Stewart 4-8-0; Hayden 2-(-1)-0; Colquitt 2-(-2)-0; Shuler 11-(-7)-0.

Passing (Comp-Att-I-Yds-TD): UA—Barker 5-11-0-54-0
UT—Shuler 12-23-1-116-1.

Receiving (Rec-Yds-TD): UA—Palmer 3-42-0; Anderson 1-4-0; Lassic 1-8-0.
UT—Faulkner 3-28-0; Fleming 2-39-0; Dabis 1-15-0; Freeman 2-12-0; Phillips 1-9-0; Stewart 1-8-0; Horn 1-3-1; Garner 1-2-0.

DEFENSIVE STATISTICS

Tackles (Primary-Assists-Total): UA—Rogers 8-0-8; Oden 4-0-4; Shade 3-1-4; Copeland 4-0-4.
UT—Ingram 9-5-14; Talley 10-2-12; McClesky 11-1-12; Parker 8-3-11.

Sacks: UA—Copeland 2 (-9); Gregory 1 (-8); Curry 1 (-4).
UT—Wilson 2 (-13); Kelly 1 (-9).

Tackles for Losses: UA—Curry 2 (-3); Copeland 1 (-3); Oden 1 (-3).
UT—McClesky 2 (-8); Kelly 1 (-8); Wilson 1 (-4).

Passes Broken Up: UA—Rogers, Shade, Hall, Donnelly (1 each).
UT—Talley 1.

Interceptions: UA—Donnelly 1. UT-none.

Fumbles Recovered: UA—none. UT-Ingram, Colquitt (1 each).

Fumbles Caused: UA—Copeland 1. UT-none.

Quarterback Pressures: UA—Copeland 4; Oden, London, Hall, Curry, Gregory (1 each).
UT—none.

SCORING SUMMARY

First Quarter
UA 7, UT 0—5:16 Derrick Lassic 1-yard run (Michael Proctor PAT) [8 plays, 46 yards, 3:35]

Second Quarter
UA 10, UT 0—13:42 Proctor 33-yard field goal [7 plays, 60 yards, 3:13]
UA 17, UT 0—8:00 Lassic 1-yard run (Proctor PAT) [11 plays, 66 yards, 4:44]
UA 17, UT 3—4:20 John Becksvoort 44-yard field goal [8 plays, 38 yards, 3:40]

Fourth Quarter
UA 17, UT 10—12:53 David Horn 3-yard pass from Heath Shuler [5 plays, 42 yards, 1:27]

Alabama passes its big test

by Clyde Bolton

KNOXVILLE, Oct. 18—It was a good moment, and Alabama's Derrick Lassic turned to the Good Book to describe it:

"On my second touchdown, the line opened it up like Moses did the Red Sea."

The Red Sea parted for Moses, but once again the Crimson Tide wouldn't part for Tennessee, and Alabama now has defeated the Volunteers for seven straight years.

A major reason for Saturday's 17-10 success was the offensive line's ability to move the Tennesseans like a road grader moving clay.

At least during the first half.

That's when Bama scored all its points. But with that murderous defense backing its play, the offense had all the scoreboard lights it needed. As Lassic said, "When Tennessee got the ball with 1:33 to play, I looked at our defense, and I knew Tennessee wasn't going to score."

Martin Houston's losing a fumble to Tennessee on its 48 at that juncture gave the Vols a last jolt of hope, but two plays later Bama's Chris Donnelly intercepted, and the defense had done it again.

Ball-hogging offense

But the offense's straight-ahead, blow-'em-out romp in the first half was a refreshing performance by an attack

A triumphant Lassic postures for his offensive linemen Tobie Sheils (61) and Roosevelt Patterson (77)

unit that has had its problems this year.

Bama had the ball 19 minutes and 27 seconds, compared to Tennessee's 10:33 in the first two periods. They rushed for 229 yards in that span, throwing only six passes. Tailback Lassic compiled a good day's work in the first half, running 24 times for 115 yards and two TDs. He finished with 142 yards in 33 tries.

Did he enjoy such a punishing assignment? "Punish me! Punish me!" Lassic said. "I love it. You can't punish me enough."

Linemen Matt Hammond, George Wilson, Tobie Sheils, Jon Stevenson and Roosevelt Patterson and playmates rumbled like characters in an ole-timey Alabama-Tennessee game, straightforward helmet busters. Wallace Wade and Gen. Neyland would have admired them.

"We felt we could run the ball on Tennessee," Lassic said. "We knew the offensive line would have to play well. We challenged them, and they responded." They say tough backs want the ball. Well, tough linemen want the ball behind them. "The linemen were saying,

'Run it behind me, run it behind me.' We were deciding which one to run it behind," offensive line coach Jimmy Fuller said.

But, with a critical coach's eye, Fuller added, "We're still struggling and making mistakes. I don't think it's ever as bad as it seems or ever as good as it seems."

Tide win silences some critics

Tennessee fans were heckling the Alabama coaches before the game.

"They were yelling, 'Who have you played? Who have you played?'" recalled offensive line coach Jimmy Fuller.

It was a reference to what some perceived as Alabama's first six opponents being soft.

Woody McCorvey, the receivers coach, looked over the Big Orange fans and quipped, "Well, we've played Arkansas."

One week previously, a three-touchdown underdog Arkansas had upset the Volunteers 25-24.

David Palmer makes a spectacular grab in a big day for receivers against Ole Miss

Don't Make Us Pass

Mississippi

Air Tide flies by Ole Miss

By Jimmy Bryan

TUSCALOOSA, Oct. 25—The Ole Miss Rebels slammed the door on Alabama's Derrick Lassic, Chris Anderson, Martin Houston and the second-best running game in the Southeastern Conference Saturday, and invited quarterback Jay Barker to beat them with a mediocre passing game.

Barker and his super-quick receivers turned mediocre into marvelous and did it.

The sophomore from Trussville used a career-best passing day to let the Crimson Tide slam Ole Miss 31-10 before a sellout crowd of 70,123 and take another giant step toward the Southeastern Conference Championship Game in Birmingham Dec. 5.

Barker threw 39 passes, completed 25 and gained 285 yards with them—all career bests. One of his passes was a 22-yard touchdown to David Palmer. Barker's previous career bests were 14 completions, 27 attempts and 192 yards.

Alabama's running game, which got 301 yards at Tennessee last week and was averaging 241 yards per game rushing, netted 83 Saturday. Lassic came in with three consecutive 100-yard games, but against Ole Miss he had 18 for eight carries.

The Tide, which was averaging 241 yards per game rushing, 11th best in the country, was held to 83 yards by Ole Miss.

Alabama's 18th consecutive win settled the Crimson Tide at 8-0 overall and 5-0 in the SEC West. More importantly, it provides a two-game lead over Mississippi State with three conference games to go.

After taking this week off, Alabama has LSU and Mississippi State on the road and Auburn in Birmingham. Two wins will make it for sure. One probably will.

Ole Miss arrived at Saturday morning's 11:40 kickoff in second place behind Alabama in the SEC West with two losses. It left at 4-3 overall, 3-3 in the SEC and out of the race.

But the Rebels threw stiff resistance at the Tide, which made it look impressive with

TOP 25 AP POLL
1. MIAMI
2. WASHINGTON
3. MICHIGAN
4. ALABAMA
5. TEXAS A&M
6. FLORIDA STATE
7. GEORGIA
8. COLORADO
9. NEBRASKA
10. NOTRE DAME
11. BOSTON COLLEGE
12. SYRACUSE
13. SOUTHERN CAL
14. PENN STATE
15. STANFORD
16. TENNESSEE
17. ARIZONA
18. KANSAS
19. WASHINGTON STATE
20. FLORIDA
21. NORTH CAROLINA STATE
22. NORTH CAROLINA
23. VIRGINIA
24. MISSISSIPPI STATE
25. TEXAS

two fourth-quarter touchdowns.

After a scoreless first quarter, Alabama pretty much put it away with a 17-point second quarter. The Tide led 17-7 at the half. After a scoreless third quarter, Bama did put it away with a 14-point fourth.

"I thought as a rule we played pretty well," Alabama coach Gene Stallings said. "Jay threw the ball well. I wasn't worried about a letdown (after an emotional 17-10 victory over Tennessee), I was worried about playing a tough team. They had two losses, but were still in it (SEC race).

"We didn't have anything to prove, but we did have a lot to play for. It was the last game here for the seniors, and we have the winning streak (18 straight victories).

"You don't have to flaunt your success, but you don't have to apologize for it, either."

Ole Miss coach Billy Brewer felt his team fired its best shots at the Crimson Tide. He felt two of Alabama's touchdowns were gifts, one after a 13-yard drive following an interception and another on a 19-yard drive after a fumble.

"We came to Tuscaloosa to play a good football team, and they are," he said, "but I think we gave away 14 points. I felt if we were going to be successful we had to play about flawless and have an outstanding kicking game.

Ole Miss showed no early respect for the Alabama offense, or defense. The Rebels stuffed Alabama's first offensive opportunity, then came wheeling down

Even some of Palmer's misses are spectacular as was this one-handed effort in the end zone

the field on their second try.

Starting at its 33, Ole Miss moved to Alabama's 32 with a first down. However, the Tide stopped it there and Brian Lee was straight but short on a 51-yard field goal.

It rocked along until Tide punter Bryne Diehl pinned Ole Miss at its 1-yard line in the second quarter. The Rebels tried to pass their way out and George Teague intercepted Russ Shows' pass at the 13.

Houston lost 2 yards and Barker was sacked for minus-8. On third-and-20, Barker hit Palmer for a touchdown. Michael Proctor's kick made it 7-0 with 12:42 left in the half.

The Tide stopped Ole Miss and started toward another touchdown from its 23 yard line. The drive went 77 yards in 11 plays, the big ones from Barker's passing. He hit Palmer for 24, Palmer for 8, Kevin Lee for 14 and 8 and Lassic finally scored on a 2-yard run.

GAME STATS AND SCORING

Alabama	0	17	0	14	31
Mississippi	0	7	0	3	10

STATISTICS	UA	UM
First Downs	22	10
Rushing (Atts/Yds)	41-83	29-109
Passing (Comp/Atts/Int)	25-39-1	8-22-1
Passing Yards	285	102
Total Offense	368	211
Average Gain Per Play	4.60	4.14
Fumbles/Lost	1-0	1-1
Total Turnovers	1	2
Punting(No/Avg)	5-46.8	6-44.3
Punt Returns(No/Yds)	5-51	3-39
Kickoff Returns(No/Yds)	2-54	5-146
Penalties/Yards	8-59	6-49
Time of Possession	37:18	22:42
Third Down Conversions	9-20	2-12
Fourth Down Conversions	2-2	1-2
Sacks/Lost	2-11	2-11

INDIVIDUAL STATISTICS

Rushing (Att-Yds-TD): UA—Lassic 8-18-1; Williams 6-15-2; Anderson 8-17-0; Houston 6-7-0; Palmer 1-8-0; Wimbley 1-5-0; Lynch 2-5-0; Barker 5-(-5)-0; Burgdorf 4-13-0.
UM—Philpot 8-31-0; Innocent 7-65-0; Courtney 4-14-0; Shows 4-3-0; Bell 3-5-0; Adams 3-(-9)-0.

Passing (Comp-Att-I-Yds-TD): UA—Barker 25-39-1-285-1.
UM—Shows 7-19-1-93-1; Adams 1-3-0-9-0.

Receiving (Rec-Yds-TD): UA—Lee 8-82-0; Palmer 7-67-1; Wimbley 3-51-0; C. Brown 3-41-0 Anderson 2-22-0; Williams 2-22-0.
UM—Small 7-101-1; Philpot 1-1-0.

DEFENSIVE STATISTICS

Tackles (Primary-Assists-Total): UA—Oden 4-5-9; Shade 5-1-6; Copeland 4-1-5; Rogers 4-1-5; Gregory 2-3-5.
UM—Jackson 6-8-14; Ware 6-6-12; Amos 8-3-11; Dixon 8-3-11.

Sacks: UA—Copeland 1 (-2); Lockett 1 (-9).
UM—Ross 2 (-11).

Tackles for Losses: UA—Copeland 2 (-3); Rogers 1 (-4).
UM—Ware 2 (-5); Jackson, Dixon, Ford (1 for -2 each).

Passes Broken Up: UA—Oden, Copeland, Langham, Donnelly (1 each).
UM—none.

Interceptions: UA—Teague 1. UM—Amos 1.

Fumbles Recovered: UA—Copeland 1. UM—none.

Fumbles Caused: UA—none. UM—none.

Quarterback Pressures: UA—Copeland, Curry (2 each); Oden, London, W. Brown (1 each).
UM—Thomas 1.

SCORING SUMMARY

Second Quarter
UA 7, UM 0—12:14 David Palmer 22-yard pass from Jay Barker (Michael Proctor PAT) [3 plays, 13 yards, 1:32]
UA 14, UM 0—2:44 Derrick 2-yard run (Proctor PAT) [11 plays, 77 yards, 5:30]
UA 14, UM 7—1:26 Eddie Small 53-yard pass from Russ Shows (Brian Lee PAT) [3 plays, 68 yards, 1:18]
UA 17, UM 7—0:06 Proctor 28-yard field goal [9 plays, 52 yards, 1:20]
Fourth Quarter
UA 24, UM 7—13:38 Sherman Williams 1-yard run (Proctor PAT) [8 plays, 49 yards, 3:18]
UA 24, UM 10—9:57 Lee 32-yard field goal [8 plays, 33 yards, 3:31]
UA 31, UM 10—1:27 Williams 4-yard run (Proctor PAT) [4 plays, 19 yards, 2:59]

A good day for Bama and Barker

by Clyde Bolton

TUSCALOOSA, Oct. 25—Alabama became a complete football team Saturday.

It grew an arm.

The defense had been as stiff as a five-dollar pair of shoes. The running game had been among the nation's best. But the passing game has been, well, just passable.

Then what to our wondering eyes should appear in the 31-10 victory over Ole Miss but Air Alabama.

Jay Barker, the sophomore quarterback from Trussville, completed 25 of 39 passes for 285 yards, all career highs. He had never completed more than 14 before, but on Saturday he had No. 15 early in the third period.

Barker is a serious-minded lad, but you could detect his delight just below the surface after the game.

"It's the first time I ever saw my wide receivers tired out there," he said. "It was like, 'Don't throw it any more.'"

Barker has been perceived as a caddy, a QB of average ability who handed off in a ground-oriented offense and who benefited from the cushion provided by one of the great defenses in the school's history. But on Saturday he was the reincarnation of Snake Stabler, Joe Namath and Steve Sloan

The Reb blitz

Was it the best game of Barker's career? "I would think so," coach Gene Stallings said. "I think it was his best game. Even though he played well against Arkansas, this was a little different defense. Jay had a good game throwing the ball and handling all the blitzes and things that happened."

The Rebels brought to Bryant-Denny Stadium a blitzing, stunting defense that relies on confusing the enemy. Alabama wasn't fooled. "I only got hit a few times," Barker said.

Ole Miss obviously didn't respect Alabama's passing game. That was a fatal mistake. "Mississippi was bringing about eight guys up to stop the run all day," Barker said. "We had lots of one-on-one coverage, and when it's like that our talented wide receivers just make my job easier."

And Barker wasn't 100 percent healthy. "I had a hurt elbow," he said. "All the guys told me after the game they were going to get their hammers out and knock on my arm."

Pitchers and catchers love to pitch and catch, and that was the game plan. Reported Kevin Lee, "Coach Stallings said, 'OK, if y'all want to catch the ball, we're going to give you the chance.'"

Lee comes on

Lee, snagging a game-high eight, was one of six Bamas who caught passes. "Jay tried to throw the ball to as many people as possible," he said. "He threw it to whoever was open. This was a big game for the receivers."

Saturday Morning Live on (and in) the air was fun, but Alabama hasn't sprouted wings. It will remain principally a running team, won't it?

"Yes," Lee said. "If you can't run the ball, you can't win. We run first and pass second. We've been winning with that, and we're going to stay with that."

The significance of this game is that it demonstrated to future opponents that the Crimson Tide can pass when it's necessary. It can complete something longer than a hand-off.

"If we want to win the national championship," Lee said, "we have to be able to do both."

This was the 18th straight victory for Alabama, and talk of a national title doesn't sound farfetched at all.

Eric Curry, Antonio London and James Gregory crush LSU; hold Bengal Tigers to 22 yards rushing in 34 tries

Bama Owns Deaf Valley

LSU

Tide tramples feisty LSU Run-happy Bama wins, looks to move up in poll

By Jimmy Bryan

BATON ROUGE, La., Nov. 8—Alabama went back to basics Saturday to dodge a bullet aimed at its undefeated season, No. 3 national ranking and 18-game winning streak.

The Crimson Tide reached back for the running game and pounded spunky LSU with it, 31-11, before 76,813 fans in Tiger Stadium. The victory sent Alabama to 9-0 overall, 6-0 in the SEC and clinched at least a tie for the SEC Western Division championship.

The Tide survived a blocked punt, safety, a half-dozen penalties for 54 yards and a half-dozen sacks of quarterback Jay Barker.

The winning streak grew to 19 games, second longest in the nation to Miami's 26, and with No. 1

Washington's loss to Arizona the Tide figures to move to No. 2 in the next Associated Press poll.

"I'm glad to get out of the game with a win," Alabama coach Gene Stallings said. "We did some things that hurt us. We got way too many penalties, got a punt blocked and let them return a kickoff to great field position in the early part of the game.

"It seemed like we were struggling all the time. I'm just pleased this football team is 9-0. I think it's an outstanding accomplishment. But we have two tough games left."

LSU (1-8 overall, 1-6 in the SEC) lost a school-record seventh straight time, and now has a school-record eight losses for the season.

"Tough loss," LSU coach Curley Hallman said opening his postgame press meeting. "It was a big win for Alabama, which still maintains all its goals. One goal we didn't reach, we didn't get out of this deep rut we're in.

"We wanted to take the game into the fourth quarter with a chance to win, and didn't accomplish that. But our guys were well prepared and gave great effort. The will to win was there. Give Alabama credit. They are an outstanding football team."

After beating Ole Miss with the passing game two weeks ago, Alabama went straight at LSU. The Tide running game netted 301 yards behind the blocking of Matt Hammond, George Wilson, Tobie Sheils, Jon Stevenson, Roosevelt Patterson, Steve Busky and friends.

Darting Chris Anderson came galloping to the rescue when starting tailback Derrick Lassic went out with a bruised shoulder in the second quarter. Lassic had gained 54 yards on nine carries in the early going.

Anderson did better. The 5-foot-8, 178-pound junior from Huntsville slashed and dodged his way to a career-best 149 yards from 15 carries and scored on one and 24-yard runs. With quarterback Jay Barker chipping in 114 yards passing on 11-of-20, the Tide gathered 415 yards of offense.

LSU netted only 22 yards rushing—it had 86, lost 64 to sacks—but passed for 217 on 22-of-35. Alabama intercepted three passes. George Teague had two,

TOP 25 AP POLL
1. MIAMI
2. ALABAMA
3. MICHIGAN
4. TEXAS A&M
5. FLORIDA STATE
6. WASHINGTON
7. NEBRASKA
8. NOTRE DAME
9. ARIZONA
10. SYRACUSE
11. FLORIDA
12. GEORGIA
13. COLORADO
14. NORTH CAROLINA STATE
15. STANFORD
16. MISSISSIPPI STATE
17. BOSTON COLLEGE
18. SOUTHERN CALIFORNIA
19. OHIO STATE
20. KANSAS
21. WASHINGTON STATE
22. PENN STATE
23. TENNESSEE
24. HAWAII
25. NORTH CAROLINA

Tommy Johnson had the other.

LSU showed no lack of confidence by winning the opening coin toss and asking for the football. The fired-up Tigers drove to a field goal, opening with back-to-back 16-yard gains. Homewood's Robert Davis ran for 16 and Jamie Howard passed to David Butler for 16 more.

When the drive stalled at the Alabama 18, Pedro Suarez kicked a 35-yarder.

Alabama matched it on its first drive. The Tide didn't have any gain of 10 yards, but reached the LSU 12 before stalling. Michael Proctor kicked a 29-yard field goal to square it 3-3.

The Tide got an immediate break. Davis couldn't handle a pitchout, and Lemanski Hall covered his fumble at the LSU 17. Four plays later, Lassic dove over from the 1-yard line. It was 10-3.

Alabama was backed to its 2-yard line when Johnson intercepted Howard's long pass. On second down, James Gillyard sacked Barker for a safety. The unusual score of 10-5 hit the board.

In the second quarter, the Tide fired an 86-yard drive in a dozen plays. The biggest thing in it was Anderson's 23-yard run. Anderson also got the TD from the 2-yard-line.

It was 17-5 at the half, although LSU got to the Alabama 3-yard-line with two downs to score. The Tigers missed a pass, and Antonio London blocked Suarez's 26-yard field goal attempt.

Alabama scored touchdowns in the third and fourth quarters, sandwiched around one by LSU.

The Tide drove 85 yards in seven plays with the second-half kickoff. After Anderson's 56-yard run, Williams scored from the 1. It was 24-5.

LSU's Rodney Young blocked Bryne Diehl's punt shortly after that, and the Tigers had it at the Bama 3. A penalty gave them new life after Howard was sacked for an 8-yard loss on third down, and Robert Toomer scored from the 3. A try for two extra points failed.

Alabama wrapped it up on Williams' 24-yard run that finished off an 84-yard drive. Proctor's final point made it 31-11.

Tide fans hope Alabama, Miami on collision course for national title

By Kevin Scarbinsky

BATON ROUGE, La., Nov. 8—This game was over everywhere but on the clock, where 1:50 remained, and in the stands, where about 150 LSU fans remained to watch 15,000 or more Alabama fans celebrate. This game was Alabama 31, LSU 11.

This game was interrupted by news on that game far away in the Arizona desert. Time stood still in the midst of a time-out. The voice came down from above.

"Here's a score," said the voice from the stadium loudspeakers. "Arizona 9, Washington 3."

The voice did not say the game was over, but the voice

Derrick Oden, George Teague and Antonio London congratulate themselves for a job well done in the 31-11 Baton Rouge victory.

could not have caused more of an uproar if it had yelled, "Fire!" They cheered, clapped, shouted and smiled on the Alabama sideline and in the Alabama stands, the red horde now occupying most of the occupied territory of Tiger Stadium.

Washington, the No. 1 team in the nation, was about to lose by a final score of 16-3. Alabama, the No. 3 team in the nation, was about to win. The poll dominoes should fall this way: idle No. 2 Miami up to No. 1, Alabama up to No. 2.

And so the voice that brought the score Saturday night set off speculation amid the celebration. If Miami can stay unbeaten and No. 1 through the rest of the regular season and Alabama can stay unbeaten and No. 2 through the rest of the regular season and the SEC championship game, Miami and Alabama will play in the Sugar Bowl on New Year's Day for the national championship.

It's true. You are not hearing voices. Alabama is on a collision course with the national championship. Howard Schnellenberger has said it many times in a deluded state about his Louisville program. But

Bama Owns Deaf Valley-LSU

Alabama has done it. Alabama has won 19 straight games. Alabama has clinched at least a tie for the SEC West title. Alabama has positioned itself to move up to No. 2 in the national rankings. And Alabama has set itself on a collision course with the national championship.

Signs point to No. 1

This game was over. Alabama linebacker Michael Rogers saw the television camera and flashed the sign, one hand up, one finger out. Alabama linebacker Antonio London saw the crowd, the red sea, and flashed the same sign. For a giddy moment, there appeared to be just one thing on the minds of everyone wearing red.

Come nightfall Sunday, only one team in the land should be ranked higher than Alabama. Come sunrise Monday, Alabama can see its way clear to the national championship. Win four games, and win it all.

"I don't want to sound cocky," linebacker Derrick Oden said. "But we're a good team. You still haven't seen our best. If we reach the final game, you'll see a great Alabama football team."

You did not see a great Alabama football team Saturday. You saw a team yield too many sacks on offense and too many third-down conversions on defense and one blocked punt on special teams, which is one too many. You do such things, Alabama coach Stallings said, "and you look like you're struggling all the time."

Not all the time. Alabama does not struggle to explain after the game because, despite its struggles, Alabama does not lose.

"Who knows what the polls will do?" Stallings said. "I'm just pleased this team is 9-0. That's an outstanding accomplishment."

Over on the bayou

This game was over on the bayou. That game was over in the desert. That other game, the one in the mind involving visions of the big celebration in the Big Easy on New Year's Night, had begun in earnest. Except in the postgame declarations of the Alabama coaches and players.

Maybe they can see from here to New Orleans, but they also see trouble in the way. They see Mississippi State. The last time Alabama took a long win streak to Mississippi State, 28 games in 1980, Alabama lost. They also see an SEC championship game in the distance.

For one moment, one finger raised can mean they're thinking of No. 1. For the rest of the week and the rest of the season, it better mean one game at a time.

"You overlook anybody," Oden said, "and you get beat. We don't look ahead."

And they don't get beat.

GAME STATS AND SCORING

Alabama	10	7	7	7	31
Louisiana State	5	0	6	0	11

STATISTICS

	UA	VU
First Downs	21	16
Rushing (Atts/Yds)	54-301	34-22
Passing (Comp/Atts/Int)	11-21-0	22-35-3
Passing Yards	114	217
Total Offense	355	239
Average Gain Per Play	4.73	3.46
Fumbles/Lost	1-0	3-1
Total Turnovers	0	4
Punting(No/Avg)	6-37.3	5-32.0
Punt Returns(No/Yds)	1-(-1)	5-58
Kickoff Returns(No/Yds)	3-58	6-137
Penalties/Yards	6-54	3-25
Time of Possession	31:29	28:31
Third Down Conversions	4-12	7-17
Fourth Down Conversions	1-1	1-1
Sacks/Lost	6-50	4-27

INDIVIDUAL STATISTICS

Rushing (Att-Yds-TD): UA—Anderson 15-149-1; Wiliams 10-69-2; Lassic 9-54-1; Palmer 4-23-0; Houston 8-31-0; Lynch 1-1-0; Barker 7-(-26)-0. LSU—Davis 8-31-0; Howard 4-11-0; G. Williams 1-2-0; Beckham 2-1-0; Toomer 4-1-1; Huffman 1-5-0; Butler 2-(-1)-0; Moore 2-(-2)-0; Loup 5-(-29)-0.

Passing (Comp-Att-I-Yds-TD): UA—Barker 11-20-0-114-0; Williams 0-1-0-0-0. LSU—Howard 14-25-3-162-0; Loup 8-10-0-55-0.

Receiving (Rec-Yds-TD): UA—Busky 1-26-0; Wimbley 4-26-0; Williams 1-24-0; C. Brown 1-14-0; Palmer 2-18-0; Anderson 2-6-0. LSU—Ray 6-63-0; Bishop 6-49-0; Jacob 4-30-0; Bech 2-30-0; Butler 1-16-0; Wilson 1-7-0; Beckham 1-6-0.

DEFENSIVE STATISTICS

Tackles (Primary-Assists-Total): UA—Rogers 6-5-11; Hall 6-4-10; London 7-1-8; Langham 4-2-6. LSU—Hilliard 3-6-11; Gillyard 3-7-10; Adams 4-3-7; White 1-5-6.
Sacks: UA—Copeland 2 (-9); Nunley 1 (-20); London 1 (-11). LSU—Washington 1 (-11); B. Williams 1 (-8); Stepteau 1 (-6); Gillyard 1 (-2).
Tackles for Losses: UA—Copeland 3 (-10); London 1 (-4); Hall 1 (-1); Nunley 1(-20); Oden 1 (-8); W. Brown 1 (-3); Gregory 1 (-2); Rogers 1 (-1). LSU—B. Williams 4 (-14); Mouton 2 (-16).
Passes Broken Up: UA—Curry, Copeland (1 each). LSU—Buckles 2, Young 1.
Interceptions: UA—Teague 2, Tom. Johnson 1. LSU—none.
Fumbles Recovered: UA—Hall 1. LSU—Hill 1.
Fumbles Caused: London 2.
Blocked Punt/Field Goal: UA—London 1. LSU—Young 1.
Quarterback Pressures: UA—Curry 3; Gregory, Copeland (1 each).

SCORING SUMMARY

First Quarter
UA 0, LSU 3—12:29 Pedro Suarez 35-yard field goal [6 plays, 37 yards, 2:25]
UA 3, LSU 3—7:27 Michael Proctor 29-yard field goal [11 plays, 62 yards, 4:46]
UA 10, LSU 3—5:49 Derrick Lassic 1-yard run (Proctor PAT) [4 plays 17 yards, 1:31]
UA 10, LSU 5—1:59 James Gillyard tackled Jay Barker in endzone
Second Quarter
UA 17, LSU 5—5:46 Chris Anderson 2-yard run (Proctor PAT) [12 plays, 86 yards, 4:58]
Third Quarter
UA 24, LSU 5—12:21 Sherman Williams 1-yard run (Proctor PAT) [7 plays, 85 yards, 2:30]
UA 24, LSU 11—7:46 Robert Toomer 1-yard run (Run failed) [3 plays, 3 yards, 1:30]
Fourth Quarter
UA 31, LSU 11—4:04 Williams 24-yard run (Proctor PAT) [11 plays, 84 yards, 5:31]

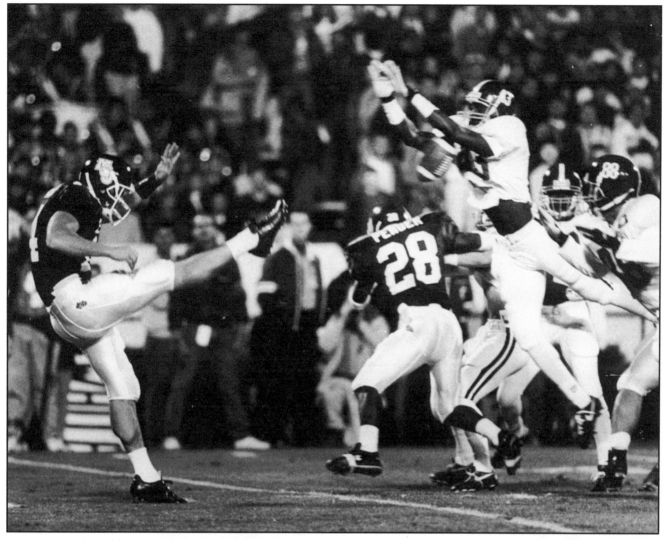

Antonio Langham blocks punt against Miss. State in a game that was too close for comfort for the Tide

A Scare in Starkville

Mississippi State

10-0 Tide knocks out State

By Jimmy Bryan

STARKVILLE, Miss., Nov. 15—Unbeaten Alabama had to rally with 10 fourth-quarter points Saturday night to beat upset-minded Mississippi State 30-21.

The victory made the Crimson Tide 10-0 and 7-0 in the Southeastern Conference, and it clinched for Alabama the SEC Western Division championship.

Antonio Langham blocked a put and returned it for a touchdown to give Alabama an early 14-0 lead, and it appeared the Tide would rout the Bulldogs.

But Jackie Sherrill's team was too good to quit despite training 20-3 at the half.

Mississippi State rallied to take a 21-20 lead on Chris Gardner's 27-yard field goal with 1:29 left in the third quarter.

But after a bizarre punt return sequence in which

both sides fumbled the ball, Alabama regained the lead on Michael Proctor's 26-yard field goal with 8:10 remaining in the fourth period.

Alabama then padded its margin after George Teague's shoestring interception gave the Tide the ball on the State 19. Five plays later, Chris Anderson scored on a 1-yard run to give Alabama a 30-21 lead with 5:13 left.

Teague picked off another pass—his 14th career interception—with 28 seconds left at the goal line to halt State's final drive.

Although Alabama's top-rated defense gave up 21 points—10 points more than any other opponent

TOP 25 AP POLL
1. MIAMI
2. **ALABAMA**
3. FLORIDA STATE
4. TEXAS A&M
5. WASHINGTON
6. MICHIGAN
7. NOTRE DAME
8. SYRACUSE
9. FLORIDA
10. GEORGIA
11. COLORADO
12. NEBRASKA
13. NORTH CAROLINA STATE
14. STANFORD
15. SOUTHERN CALIFORNIA
16. ARIZONA
17. OHIO STATE
18. MISSISSIPPI STATE
19. BOSTON COLLEGE
20. TENNESSEE
21. NORTH CAROLINA
22. KANSAS
23. PENN STATE
24. MISSISSIPPI
25. WAKE FOREST

has scored this season—the Tide managed to hand the Bulldogs their first home loss this year before a sellout crowd at chilly Scott Stadium

Charlie Davidson's interception on the third play of the second half triggered the comeback by Mississippi State.

Two plays after Davidson's interception, Orlanda Truitt made a diving, one-handed grab of a tipped pass in the end zone for a State touchdown.

Greg Plump then passed to tight end Curt Clanton for the two-point conversion, cutting Alabama's lead to 21-11.

After forcing Alabama to punt, Mississippi State drove 47 yards and scored on a 1-yard dive by Plump to make it 20-18.

State, which has lost 34 of its last 35 games against Alabama, finally took the lead on Gardner's field goal late in the third quarter. The Bulldogs had a first-and-goal at the Alabama 1, but were penalized 15 yards for having an extra man on the field, and were forced to settle for the field goal.

Miss. State's quarterback suffered under the surge of Antonio London and John Copeland just as many others had

Alabama scored the first time it had the ball on a 23-yard shovel pass from Jay Barker to Derrick Lassic. Two minutes later, the Tide increased its lead to 14-0 when Langham blocked Todd Jordan's punt, picked it up on the Bulldog's 5 and run it into the end zone.

It was Langham's second career touchdown on a blocked punt return.

He also did it against Vanderbilt in 1990.

The Tide made it 17-0 when Proctor kicked a 41-yard field goal on the third play of the second period, capping a 10-play, 55-yard drive.

Each team lost a fumble on the next possessions, but neither side could capitalize.

Gardner, who missed a 42-yard field goal attempt in the first quarter, booted a 37-yarder with 5:53 left in the half to make it 17-3.

A sensational catch by Kevin Lee set up a 21-yard field goal by Proctor on the final play of the half, giving Alabama a 20-3 lead.

Lee and cornerback Edward Williams jumped for the long pass from Barker, the ball popped in the air, and Lee caught it at the State 4 while falling to the ground.

GAME STATS AND SCORING

Alabama	14	6	0	10	30
Mississippi State	0	3	18	0	21

STATISTICS	UA	MSU
First Downs	18	18
Rushing (Atts/Yds)	50-106	39-114
Passing (Comp/Atts/Int)	13-28-2	15-30-2
Passing Yards	198	187
Total Offense	304	301
Average Gain Per Play	3.90	4.40
Fumbles/Lost	2-1	4-2
Total Turnovers	3	4
Punting(No/Avg)	5-36.0	4-24.3
Punt Returns(No/Yds)	2-27	5-74
Kickoff Returns(No/Yds)	0-0	5-62
Penalties/Yards	2-10	6-
Time of Possession	32:00	28:00
Third Down Conversions	9-18	3-12
Fourth Down Conversions	0-1	0-2
Sacks/Lost	2-16	3-30

INDIVIDUAL STATISTICS

Rushing (Att-Yds-TD): UA—Anderson 12-51-1; Lassic 15-29-0; Williams 9-29-0; Palmer 5-23-0; Lynch 2-2-0; Houston 1-5-0; Lee 1-(-2)-0; Barker 5-(-31)-0.
MSU—Davis 13-54-0; Brown 4-20-0; Roberts 6-18-0; Prince 2-13-0; McCrary 2-5-0; Plump 11-3-1; Hudson 1-1-0.
Passing (Comp-Att-I-Yds-TD): UA—Barker 13-27-2-198-1; Palmer 0-1-0-0-0.
MSU—Plump 14-28-2-193; Hudson 1-1-0-(-6)-0; Truitt 0-1-0-0-0.
Receiving (Rec-Yds-TD): UA—Lee 4-81-0; Wimbley 3-58-0; Lassic 2-31-0; C. Brown 2-23-0; Houston 1-2-0; Busky 1-3-0.
MSU—W. Harris 4-72-0; Truitt 3-44-1; Clanton 3-40-0; Roberts 3-27-0; Davis 2-4-0.

DEFENSIVE STATISTICS

Tackles (Primary-Assists-Total): UA—Hall 7-8-15; Shade 6-4-10; Tom. Johnson 8-1-9; Rogers 7-1-8; Oden 6-2-8.
MSU—Woodard 9-4-13; Long 6-5-11; Henry 7-3-10.
Sacks: UA—Curry 1 (-8); Hall 1 (-8).
MSU—Henry 3 (-30).
Tackles for Losses: UA—Oden 1 (-5); Hall 1 (-3); Rogers 1 (-1).
MSU—Woodard 3 (-9); Boyd 1 (-3).
Passes Broken Up: UA—London 2; Teague, Langham, E. Brown (1 each).
MSU—none.
Interceptions: UA—Teague 2. MSU—Davidson 2.
Fumbles Recovered: UA—Teague, Bevelle (1 each). MSU—Curtis, Knight (1 each).
Fumbles Caused: UA—none. MSU—none.
Blocked Punt: UA—Teague 1.
Quarterback Pressures: UA—Copeland 2; Curry, W. Brown, Hall (1 each).

SCORING SUMMARY

First Quarter
UA 7, MSU 0 - 9:40 Derrick Lassic 23-yard pass from Jay Barker (Michael Proctor PAT) [7 plays, 67 yards, 3:09]
UA 14, MSU 0 - 7:39 Antonio Langham 24-yard blocked-punt return (Proctor PAT) [1 play, 5 yards, :03]
Second Quarter
UA 17, MSU 0 - 13:30 Proctor 41-yard field goal [10 plays, 51 yards, 4:47]
UA 17, MSU 3 - 5:53 Chris Gardner 37-yard field goal [6 plays, 16 yards, 3:23]
UA 20, MSU 3 - 0:00 Proctor 21-yard field goal [6 plays, 59 yards, :54]
Third Quarter
UA 20, MSU 11 - 13:30 Olanda Truitt 10-yard pass from Greg Plump (Plump to Curt Clanton 2-point conv.) [2 plays, 11 yards, :40]
UA 20, MSU 18 - 9:27 Plump 1-yard run (Gardner PAT) [7 plays, 47 yards, 3:02]
UA 20, MSU 21 - 1:30 Gardner 27-yard field goal [12 plays, 46 yards, 4:42]
Fourth Quarter
UA 23, MSU 21 - 8:10 Proctor 26-yard field goal [9 plays, 34 yards, 3:20]
UA 30, MSU 21 - 5:13 Chris Anderson 1-yard run (Proctor PAT) [5 plays, 19 yards, 1:57]

Auburn's defense was tough, but Alabama's was tougher as Stan White can attest. Trainers work on the Auburn QB who suffered a separated shoulder late in the game.

Iron Bowl—Iron Defense

Auburn

The Iron Bowl

Iron Bowl week began with Alabama shaking off the brief scare at Mississippi State, while a beleaguered Pat Dye professed to be planning a long stay as Auburn's head coach.

All season long Dye continually caught splatters from the mudslinging of Eric Ramsey, his former player who claimed he got extra benefits in violation of NCAA rules while at Auburn.

The formal NCAA letter of allegations had arrived, and Dye was named specifically in at least one, charging him with knowing about violations and not reporting it.

His team was struggling on the field and, while fielding a tough defense, could not seem to find the offensive combination to mount consistent threats.

Still, Auburn was dangerous—a formidable foe astride the road to a national championship bid.

At the same time, Alabama players were going through some self analysis brought on by the close shave in Starkville.

In a single quarter, Mississippi State had scored as many points on Alabama as the Crimson Tide had allowed all the year in the first half.

"What can I say? We lost our poise in the third quarter," said linebacker Antonio London. "That was the biggest disappointment about...the Mississippi State game...

"Giving up 21 points doesn't bother us as much as losing our poise."

"We need to start playing like the No. 1 defense from here on out," said senior end Eric Curry, a Lombardi Award finalist. "The Mississippi State game let us know we're not Supermen...we're not invincible."

As Iron Bowl week wore on, teams jockeyed for psychological position. Tide seniors recalled the 1989 team, ranked No. 2 in the country, but losing 30-20 in Jordan-Hare Stadium. "We win the game and we play Miami for the national championship in the Sugar Bowl.

"We still went to the Sugar, but Auburn took our national championship drams away. It was a devastating loss," recalled George Teague.

On the other side, Dye put his best country-tough foot forward: "We've tried mighty hard to get our football team to improve to the point that going into this last game we would have a chance to win the game.

"And I think we've got a chance."

Auburn's psychological bombshell was to come on the very eve of the game. Despite assurances only days earlier that he would be coaching at Auburn for years to come, Pat Dye tendered his resignation.

How would the event affect the Auburn players. Would they burn with an emotional fever to win the last one for their beloved coach? Was this to be the hole in the road to Alabama's championship?

The answer, we know now of course, is no. Auburn fought gallantly. And there were tears of sympathy for the resigned coach. There even was an emotional moment between the two warriors—Dye and Stallings—with the Alabama coach consoling and supporting his cross-state adversary.

TOP 25 AP POLL
1. MIAMI
2. ALABAMA
3. FLORIDA STATE
4. TEXAS A&M
5. NOTRE DAME
6. SYRACUSE
7. MICHIGAN
8. GEORGIA
9. COLORADO
10. WASHINGTON
11. NEBRASKA
12. FLORIDA
13. NORTH CAROLINA STATE
14. STANFORD
15. OHIO STATE
16. BOSTON COLLEGE
17. TENNESSEE
18. WASHINGTON STATE
19. MISSISSIPPI
20. NORTH CAROLINA
21. PENN STATE
22. ARIZONA
23. SOUTHERN CALIFORNIA
24. MISSISSIPPI STATE
25. BRIGHAM YOUNG

If sympathy wins ballgames, this one would have gone to the Tigers, hands down.

But victory goes to the strong. And on Thursday, Nov. 26, 1992, the Crimson Tide was the strongest.

Bama's mighty defense marches on

By Jimmy Bryan

BIRMINGHAM, Nov. 27—The University of Alabama's second-ranked football team proved conclusively Thanksgiving afternoon that great talent is a more powerful fuel than emotion.

The Crimson Tide peeled away the emotion of Auburn coach Pat Dye's shocking Wednesday night resignation to punish the Tigers with a 17-o Iron Bowl shutout at Legion Field Thursday afternoon. A sellout crowd of 83,091 and a national television audience looked on.

It was the first shutout ever of a Dye-coached team.

Winning this most bitter of rivalries for the third straight year would normally be satisfaction enough for Alabama. Particularly when it means an undefeated regular season of 11-0 and extension of a winning streak to 21 in a row.

Yet Thursday's victory advances Alabama tantalizingly within reach of more significant things.

The Crimson Tide moves into the first-ever SEC Championship Game at Legion Field against Florida a week from Saturday unblemished and looking for a national championship.

If the Tide handles Florida, the stage will be set for a Sugar Bowl showdown with No. 1 Miami New Year's Day. The Hurricanes have only out-classed San Diego State Saturday in the way of holding their No. 1 ranking.

Alabama coach Gene Stallings refused any national championship discussion.

"We've won 11 games and still haven't won any-

Auburn defenders were after Bama QB Jay Barker all day

thing," he said late Thursday afternoon. "I have no thoughts on anybody but the University of Florida. We've been able to concentrate (on the next game) well all year.

"We still haven't played our best game. Maybe we will next week."

Dye, in a final press conference as Auburn coach that became emotionally-charged, paid tribute to his main rival of the past 12 years.

"This was a great day for Coach Stallings, the Alabama players and fans," Dye said. "If I had a vote for No. 1, Alabama would get my vote."

The Crimson Tide defense stuffed Auburn with a net of only 20 yards rushing and 119 passing. It was Bama's third shutout of the season, but first over Auburn since 1975 (28-0).

The Alabama defense celebrates early success against the Tigers

But Auburn played the 15 1/2-point favored Crimson Tide to a 0-0 standoff in the first half. It was perhaps fitting the game was turned early in the second half by Alabama's No. 1-in-the-nation defense.

Auburn was proceeding on its most productive drive of the game. It had put together two first downs under its own power for the first time, and moved 36 yards to the Alabama 39.

On second-and-6, Tide cornerback Antonio Langham stepped in front of receiver Orlando Parker and tipped quarterback Stan White's pass in the air. He gathered it in and fled 61 yards for the game's first points.

"Man, I can't explain it," Langham said. "We were in a man-to-man and the receiver ran an out. I saw it coming. I reached out, tipped it and all I saw was green. I wasn't worried about anything else."

Parker said he felt he had a chance to catch the pass.

"He (Langham) was lined up on top of me," Parker said. "I ran a two-step out. He stepped right in front of me. I didn't see him coming. I was looking at the ball, waiting to catch it. He tipped it and then caught it.

"I thought I had a good chance to catch him, but somebody knocked me about 10 yards out of bounds. I believe I could have caught him."

Giving chase were offensive tackle Wayne Gandy and White. Neither came close.

"I know no adjective to describe how big that play was," said Stallings. "I always tell our players they play 55 or 66 plays for the privilege to make one or two."

Following the touchdown, Auburn made one first down and had to punt again. Terry Daniels" first effort was a 51-yarder that pinned the Tide at its 11-yard line. However, Auburn was penalized for holding and the next effort was only 37 yards.

Alabama took off from its 40 instead of its 11. Quarterback Jay Barker hit a third-and-5 pass of 20 yards to Curtis Brown at the Auburn 35. When the

Eric Curry closes in on Auburn QB Stan White who was under pressure all day

Tide reached the 21, the Tiger defense knocked it back 9 yards.

Michael Proctor's field goal was lengthened to 47 yards, but he got it home with a helping wind. It was 10-0 with the third quarter ending in three minutes.

"The interception return on our first drive of the second half hurt," Dye said. "And then they got the field goal. But 10-0 is not a big lead unless you've got a defense like Alabama. Then it's a monumental lead."

When Alabama scored in the fourth quarter on a 45-yard drive after Daniels' only bad punt, a 16-yard shank, everybody knew it was over.

Players helped Gene Stallings celebrate with a cold shower, something that became a more and more popular game- ending event as the season wore on

Quick little Sherman Williams did the final damage on a 15-yard run with 12:08 left in the game.

Auburn attempted to dodge the shutout when White moved his troops to the Alabama 30. However, he was injured and backup Patrick Nix couldn't take the Tigers any closer.

Scott Etheridge missed a 48-yard field goal attempt with 4:26 remaining and Auburn never got the ball back.

Auburn's defense left all it had on the field. The Tide netted 199 yards rushing, but only 63 passing. Each team had three turnovers, a fumble and two interceptions.

Dye and Stallings meet in emotional moment

Cameras flashed as Alabama coach Gene Stallings placed his arm around Auburn coach Pat Dye and

A grim Stallings scowls from the sideline

It was a tough day for defenses and offenses in a fierce Iron Bowl struggle

embraced his rival Thursday in the pre-game warm-ups at Legion Field.

Stallings and Dye have never been close friends in the profession, but they have been soldiers fighting the same wars every Saturday in the fall.

They have been enemies, yet they have shared common ground.

This would be the last time the two old warriors would meet in battle, the last time Dye would coach an Auburn team against Stallings in the Iron Bowl.

For this, they said their good-byes.

"It was really sad," Stallings recalled after No. 2 Alabama defeated its archrival 17-0 at Legion Field before a capacity crowd of 83,091. "I told him we would miss him. I told him college football would miss him. It was probably more of an emotional meet-

Auburn coach Pat Dye tips his hat to the crowd as he leaves after coaching his final game against Alabama

ing than I was expecting."

While they embraced, while they put their arms around each other and spoke to their ears only, Dye's Auburn cap tumbled off his head.

Without the cap, without the security of something that could hide the eyes, Dye's emotions were exposed.

There were tears in his eyes and Stallings could feel the emotions running through Dye.

There was a lump in Stallings' throat.

"I told him how I felt," Stallings said. "I just hate to see him leave the game like that.

"I don't know about the NCAA problems," Stallings said. "But I feel for Pat, his family, his coaches and his players."

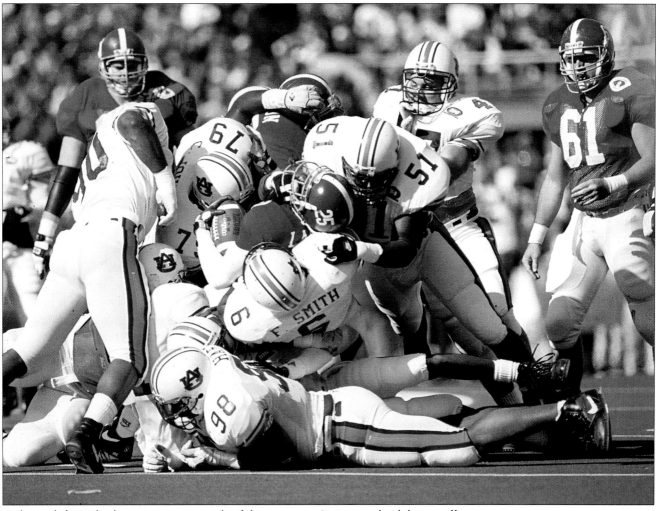

Auburn defense had great success much of the game against a tough Alabama offense

Stallings wearing his success well

by Clyde Bolton

Gene Stallings has a perfect record as Alabama's football coach this season, but no matter what he does he'll never be Alabama's perfect football coach. That position is already filled.

Stallings ducked into the bathroom of a local restaurant Monday, and a man followed him. "Who called them plays in the third quarter?" the fellow demanded, referring to the close call against Missis-sippi State Saturday night.

"Well, I'll tell you one thing," the man sniffed. "The Bear would never have done that."

Stallings loved it. He delighted in telling the story. He has never had any illusions about "replacing" the Bear. I am reminded of his great line: "Alabama fans love coach Bryant and tolerate the rest of us."

But Stallings is mighty easy to tolerate these days. His Crimson Tide is 10-0. It has won 20 straight games. Stallings lost his first three games as Bryant's heir, but his record in three seasons at Tuscaloosa is 28-6.

Can change quickly

But it's the nature of the beast that last week's cheers blend into this week's moans of concern. The road behind may be smooth, but the one ahead could have potholes, what with the Iron Bowl game against Auburn, the SEC title match and a bowl on the horizon.

Stallings reflected: "I told my wife, 'Last year we won 11 games, and this year we're 10-0, and we haven't won anything yet.' Oh, we won the division, whatever that is. But you'd think we would have at least won the conference."

He's serious about winning, but he recognizes the humor in what he does. Saturday night, during the game at Starkville, he complained to an official about the fans:

"I'm tired of those so-and-sos throwing at me. A guy hit me in the head with a nickel."

"Where is it?" the official asked.

"It's in my pocket," Stallings answered. "You want it?"

"Yeah, I want it," the official said. "I'll put it in my collection."

Stallings said he wasn't worried about giving money to an official because you can't buy a ballgame for five cents.

Some of the happenings in this strange profession that he has followed for decades chap him. Tennessee's decision to buy out Coach Johnny Majors' contract "makes me sad," he said.

"Johnny Majors is a friend of mine, and he has been for a long time. Here was a guy who was an All-American at Tennessee and came back from a heart attack...and they don't let him even finish the year without talking about buying up his contract. You don't know how embarrassing that is."

Offered Stallings: "It makes you wonder why anybody would want to be in college coaching.

Wins with defense

Nobody wants to buy out Stallings' contract. His team makes the other side punt, and the other side can't score when it's punting.

"We are by far the best third-down defensive team I've ever seen," Stallings said in the traditional address of the Alabama football coach to the Monday Morning Quarterback Club. "We are dominant because few people convert on us on third down."

There are three things a football team must do to win games, Stallings said, and Alabama does all three. They are the same three factors he cited his team for accomplishing last year.

A club must be able to play defense, run the football and excel in giveaway-takeaway.

"That's why we are winning ball games," he said. "We are struggling in some areas, but we are not beating ourselves."

GAME STATS AND SCORING

Alabama	0	0	10	7	17
Auburn	0	0	0	0	0

STATISTICS

	UA	AU
First downs	17	8
Rushing (Att/Yds)	51-199	28-20
Passing (Comp/Atts/Int)	5-14-2	14-25-2
Passing Yards	63	119
Total Offense	262	139
Average Gain Per Play	4.03	2.62
Fumbles/Lost	1-1	3-1
Total Turnovers	3	3
Punting (No/Avg)	5-38.8	8-42.4
Punt Returns(No/Yds)	4-14	4-17
Kickoff Returns(No/Yds)	1-13	4-77
Penalties/Yards	7-44	8-74
Time of Possession	32:08	27:52
Third Down Conversions	6-15	3-14
Fourth Down Conversions	1-1	1-1
Sacks/Lost	5-47	1-6

INDIVIDUAL STATISTICS

Rushing (Att-Yds-TD): UA—Houston 14-68-0; Lassic 17-43-0; Williams 7-42-1; Anderson 5-19-0; Lynch 3-14-0; Barker 2-6-0; Palmer 2-5-0; Harris 1-2-0
AU—Bostic 15-55-0;McMilion 2-1-0; Yarbrough 1-0-0; White 10-(-36)-0
Passing (Comp-Att-Int-Yds-TD): UA—Barker 5-13-2-63-0; Palmer 0-1-0-0-0
AU—White 14-23-2-119-0; Nix 0-2-0-0-0
Receiving (Rec-Yds-TD): UA—C. Brown 2-41-0; Palmer 2-22-0; Lassic 1-0-0
AU—Bailey 3-46-0; Bostic 3-22-0; Sanders 2-22-0; Carder 1-11-0; McMilion 1-7-0; Richardson 1-5-0; Parker 2-3-0; Dorn 1-3-0

DEFENSIVE STATISTICS

Tackles (Primary-Assists-Total): UA—Copeland 5-3-8; Curry 4-3-7; Donnelly 2-5-7; Shade 6-1-7
AU—Willis 8-4-12; Shelling 10-1-11; Harris 8-3-11; Smith 5-4-9
Sacks: UA—Curry 2(-24); Copeland 1(-11); W. Brown 1(-8); E. Brown 1(-4)
AU—Merchant 1(-6)
Tackles for losses: UA—Rogers 1 (-3); Oden 1(-1)
AU—Willis 2(-5); Cunningham 1(-16); Johnson 1(-3); Harris 1(-3)
Passes Broken Up: UA—Copeland 1; Teague 1
AU—Jackson
Interceptions:UA—Langham 1; Tommy Johnson 1
AU—Harris 1; Smith 1
Fumbles Recovered: UA—Shade 1
AU—Cunningham 1
Fumbles Caused: UA—Teague
AU—Harris
Quarterback Pressures: UA—Curry 4; Copeland 2; Nunley 1; Hall 1
AU—Sutton 1

SCORING SUMMARY

First Quarter
UA 0, AU 0
Second Quarter
UA 0, AU 0
Third Quarter
UA 7, AU 0—11:41 Antonio Langham 61-yard interception return (Proctor kick)
UA 10, AU 0—3:04 Proctor 47-yard field goal (10 plays, 31 yards, 5:16)
Fourth Quarter
UA 17, AU 0—12:08 Sherman Williams 15-yard run (Proctor kick) (7 plays, 45 yards, 3:27)

Antonio Langham's interception and TD run late in the fourth quarter clinched Alabama's SEC championship

Conference Champions

Florida

Tide gets ready for Gators, title game

By Charles Hollis

TUSCALOOSA, Nov. 30—There has been no time to stop and savor their success.

The Alabama coaches were in their offices Friday morning—the day after Alabama beat Auburn 17-0—to prepare for their biggest game of the year, the inaugural SEC Championship Game against the Florida Gators.

The game matching SEC West champ Alabama and SEC East champ Florida at Legion Field is televised nationally.

As big as the Auburn game was, improving Alabama to 11-0, coach Gene Stallings said, "The only game that matters is the conference championship game. I know it might sound strange, but we've won 11 games and haven't won anything yet. Now we've got to turn around and play Florida and they've got a Heisman candidate at quarterback (Shane Matthews), plus an outstanding running back (Errict Rhett) and all those receivers.

"We'll be tested on defense, I'm certain about that.

Florida's an outstanding football team. They'd won seven in a row.

The Gators' winning streak came to an end Saturday when they were blasted by Florida State 45-24.

Stallings said there was no time to enjoy his team's third straight win over Auburn, which makes Stallings 3-0 with his big rival.

"I'm not going to gloat over that," Stallings said. "You're only as good as your last game."

Stallings and his coaches spent the day after the Auburn victory watching films of Florida. School was out and players were gone, many of them home with their families catching up on the Thanksgiving they missed.

TOP 25 AP POLL
1. MIAMI
2. **ALABAMA**
3. FLORIDA STATE
4. TEXAS A&M
5. NOTRE DAME
6. SYRACUSE
7. MICHIGAN
8. GEORGIA
9. WASHINGTON
10. COLORADO
11. NEBRASKA
12. FLORIDA
13. NORTH CAROLINA STATE
14. STANFORD
15. OHIO STATE
16. BOSTON COLLEGE
17. TENNESSEE
18. WASHINGTON STATE
19. MISSISSIPPI
20. NORTH CAROLINA
21. PENN STATE
22. ARIZONA
23. SOUTHERN CALIFORNIA
24. MISSISSIPPI STATE
25. BRIGHAM YOUNG

The Thanksgiving Day game enabled Stallings and his staff to get a jump on their opponent, even though the Crimson Tide will not take the practice field until today, the same time the Gators begin their preparations for the title game.

"I think our players are glad they have the opportunity to play against Florida," said Stallings. "I think our staff is glad to have another opportunity to play against Florida."

The SEC champion heads for the Sugar Bowl on New Year's Day. If it is Alabama, the likely opponent will be top-ranked Miami and the national championship will be at stake.

Stallings watched Saturday's

Derrick Lassic just makes it into the corner of the end zone for his second TD against the Gators

Coach Gene Stallings explains defensive strategy to linebacker Derrick Oden

Florida-Florida State game and the Miami-San Diego State game.

"We may never get to the Sugar Bowl and play Miami, or Miami may not get to the Sugar Bowl, but you've got to be prepared," Stallings said.

Alabama players look at the SEC championship game as a rematch of last year's contest in Gainesville that Florida won 35-0.

"We don't think Florida was 35 points better than us," said outside linebacker Antonio London. "We don't think we played the type of football this team can play. Florida's a good ball club, but we think we're a good football team.

"And we have a lot at stake."

Tide takes down Gators Sugar Bowl next for 12-0 Alabama

By Jimmy Bryan

BIRMINGHAM, Dec. 5—One last time in 1992, Alabama did what it had to do to finish a perfect season and win a shot at the national championship.

The Crimson Tide beat Florida 28-21 in the first SEC Championship Game, a game that rose to the definition of its name for a sellout crowd of 83,091 at Legion Field.

With the finished product of 12-0 safely put away, No. 2 Alabama takes the SEC's automatic Sugar Bowl bid to New Orleans on New Year's to meet No. 1 Miami for the national championship.

Alabama paved the road to Championship Weekend in Birmingham week after week with defense. And when the season of 1992 was piled on the table by the aroused Gators with three minutes to go, defense did it again.

Cornerback Antonio Langham dramatically took

Rogers, Copeland and company hold Florida offense in check in the early going

the role of Gator executioner. He intercepted quarterback Shane Matthews' pass and ran it 27 yards for the winning touchdown with 3:39 remaining in the game.

Langham won himself a prominent place in Alabama football history by providing the game-turning play for the second big game in a row. One week earlier, the junior cornerback broke up the Auburn game with a 61-yard interception for what proved to be winning points. Saturday's was a shorter but more important version. Florida appeared to have snatched momentum from the Tide by rallying from a 21-7 deficit to a 21-21 tie. The Gators had field position and 10-15 mph wind at their back.

Then Langham stepped in front of a sideline pass route, picked the ball and raced to the end zone.

"We were in a zone defense where I play the flat," Langham explained. "They had been running that little hitch route all day. This time, I played it a little differently. I squatted behind the receiver so (Shane) Matthews couldn't see me.

"I don't think he ever saw me. When he released the pass, I broke on the ball. I knew I had it. I had a little flashback to last week. You play football to make a great play. to make it for a touchdown is a cornerback's dream."

Florida took the opening kickoff 77 yards in 11 plays, and Matthews was 6-for-6 passing. He took all but 10 yards through the air to make it 7-0 Gators. The touchdown was a 5-yard shovel pass to Errict Rhett.

Now Alabama grabbed the ball and went right to

its game plan. The Tide battered 72 yards in 10 plays and 9 of them were runs. Tailback Derrick Lassic ran 7 of the 9 on the way to a quick 7-7 tie. The touchdown was a 3-yard run by Lassic.

Alabama crossed up the Gators' defense with its second touchdown. Quarterback Jay Barker got 1-on-1 coverage on the outside and hit Curtis Brown with a 30-yard scoring pass. Now Alabama led 14-7 and that was the half-time score.

They went almost 10 minutes into the third quarter before Bama hit the scoreboard again. And again it was a pass that did most of the damage. Barker caught the Gators flatfooted on first down from the Tide 34. He hit David Palmer for 39 yards to the Florida 27.

Now Alabama went back to what it does best and three runs later Lassic ran 15 yards to a touchdown and the lead was 21-7.

Florida forgot the run and went back to its bread and butter to get it tied. Matthews threw a 4-yard touchdown pass to Willie Jackson to cut the lead to 21-14 after three quarters. Then Rhett scored on a 1-yard run to tie the game at 21-all with 8:09 remaining.

Langham's interception gave the Tide its winning margin.

But Alabama's defense had one final big play waiting. With Florida attempting to come back, Matthews' pass was batted up and Michael Rogers intercepted at the Florida 48.

The Gators had one final try from 90 yards away with less than a minute to play, but failed.

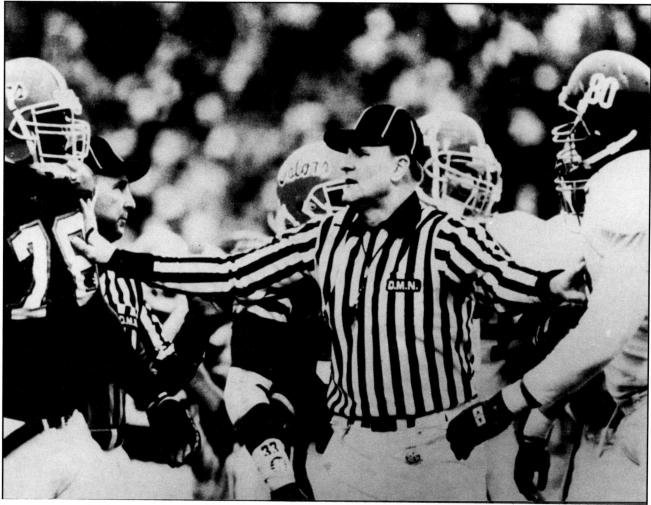

Emotions were high as seen here with a referee separating Eric Curry from a Florida offensive lineman

It's one pass too many
for Florida. One pass.

What was one pass to Shane Matthews? What was one pass to the senior quarterback who had thrown 1,193 passes in his Florida career to that moment, more passes than any quarterback in the Southeastern Conference had ever thrown in a career?

One pass. What was one pass to the two-time SEC Player of the Year? What was one pass to the player who had completed more passes for more touchdowns in his career than any quarterback in SEC history? What was one pass to the senior who had thrown 40 passes on the day to that moment into the teeth of the best pass defense in America without throwing an interception?

One pass. Before Matthews threw it, the SEC Championship Game was tied 21-21 with little more

than three minutes left to play. Before Matthews threw it, Florida had first down at its 21-yard line and more than three minutes on the clock to move to victory. Before Matthews threw it, the ball and the game and the Sugar Bowl and the national championship hopes of his opponent, Alabama, and his chief rival, Florida State, were in his hands.

And then he threw the pass. And then the ball and the game and the Sugar Bowl and the national championship hopes of Alabama and Florida State were in the hands of Alabama cornerback Antonio Langham. And then Langham, a thief in the night, was in the end zone and the game was over. It wasn't finished, but it was over.

One pass. What was one pass to the one man who has thrown more passes to the right hands than anyone else in league history? It was the difference between possible victory and certain defeat. It was the difference between Alabama playing Miami in the Sugar Bowl for the national championship and Florida State playing Miami in the Fiesta Bowl for the national championship. It was the difference between the spoils going to the victor and the victor spoiling everything for almost everyone in the house.

"It was a great football game," Matthews said. "It came down to one play. They made the play and won the game."

He was denied

One pass. Matthews would throw eight more passes after that one pass, 49 in all. One more would be intercepted. None would reach the end zone. None would overcome the one pass that meant the game.

"We played right there with the No. 2 team in the nation," Matthews said, head down, arms crossed. "I just hate to see us lose on a play like that. I feel I let the guys down."

He couldn't have been more off target. Matthews and his teammates disappointed no one. They pushed Alabama closer to the edge of defeat than anyone in the last two seasons since Florida was the last team to beat the Tide. No one in the last 21 games had come that close to Alabama that close to the end of a game.

With little more than three minutes to play, Florida stood even with Alabama. Overtime loomed. Disaster loomed for everyone from the home fans to the home-state team to a conference in desperate need of a national championship team to a bowl in desperate need of a national championship game.

But Langham loomed, just behind the receiver, just in the nick of time.

"It's going to take us a while to get over this one," Matthews said, head still down, arms still crossed. "I can tell you that."

Title game a good thing

It should not take long for everyone to see that the SEC Championship Game is the best thing to happen to college football since the forward pass. If Alabama had been able to advance to the Sugar Bowl without playing either Florida or Georgia, its championship would have been tainted.

Instead Alabama proved it is the best team in the league and dispelled any doubt that it deserves its trip to New Orleans. Florida proved it deserved its trip to

Birmingham and served notice that any future SEC champion will have to go through the Gators. It says here that Alabama and Florida will dance again in this pale moonlight any number of times before this decade is done.

Matthews won't be dancing again anytime soon. His injured toe throbbed, yet still he completed more passes for more yards against Alabama than any quarterback since Matthews himself helped beat Alabama more than a year ago.

"The toe hurts, but it had nothing to do with the way I played," Matthews said. "I would chop my toe off to have a win."

Emotional Stallings 'very proud'

By Charles Hollis

In the middle of the Alabama dressing room, as players and coaches celebrated beating Florida 28-21 and winning the first Southeastern Conference Championship Game Saturday at Legion Field, it was time to take a bow.

That's what SEC commissioner Roy Kramer told the Alabama players.

"There has never been a team in this conference to finish the regular season 12-0 and win nine conference games," Kramer said. "I told them they will always remember this day because they won the first championship game."

"To win 12 straight games is almost an impossible task, yet Alabama did win 12 games."

There was emotion in the eyes and in the voice of Alabama coach Gene Stallings as he tried to put everything in perspective.

To go 12-0, to win nine league games, to win the first SEC title game, to come back from a 21-21 tie in the fourth quarter, it had the 57-year-old Texan on top of the world and, at the same time, in awe of what his team had done.

"I feel very proud, I know that," said Stallings. "We're glad to be representing our school and conference in the Sugar Bowl. We had goals at the beginning of the year and winning our conference and going

Tackle Roosevelt Patterson with Derrick Lassic, jubilant after scoring one of his two touchdowns against the Gators

Florida was as deflated as this gator that hung from the goalpost at the end of the game. The scoreboard tells the story.

to the Sugar Bowl was one of them.

"Before the season started I felt we could have a good football team. I felt we would be a good team because we were going to be good, defensively.

"I thought it would be almost impossible for us to go 12-0, but it took every one of those wins to put us in position to play for the national championship. That was one of our goals too."

And now Alabama's fate is in the hands of the 62 Associated Press voters. When the poll is realeased today and the bowl pairings are announced on a special edition of ESPN this morning at 9, Stallings will learn whether his team will play top-ranked Miami (11-0) or No. 5 Notre Dame (9-1-1) in the Sugar Bowl.

Under guidelines set by the new bowl coalition, if No. 3 Florida State moves past No. 2 Alabama in the poll, the Fiesta Bowl would get No. 1 vs. No. 2 in a national championship game.

The Sugar would get the highest ranked team after FSU, which would be No. 5 Notre Dame.

"I don't have any control on what happens in the poll, but if I remember right didn't Florida State lose a game earlier this year? And let's see. Aren't we 12-0 and No. 2 in the nation?

"I hope we get the opportunity to play Miami. I would expect that's what will happen. I think it would be a great game. Miami with its (28-game) winning streak and our 22-game winning streak."

An Associated Press editor said Saturday night from his New York office, where the poll will be released from, that it will take half of the voters to change their votes for FSU to move ahead of Alabama.

"I think it will be close," said the AP editor who asked not to be named. "But I think Alabama will end up No.2, ahead of Florida State. But it's not cut and dried. It's going to be a close vote."

The vote was expected to be close because of Florida State's 21-point victory over archrival Florida and Alabama's 7-point win Saturday over Florida.

If voters compare the scores of the two games, there was a feeling be reporters covering Saturday's SEC Championship Game that Alabama could get leap-frogged.

"I just don't think it's going to happen," Stallings said. "I think when people look at our record and what we've done, we'll stay No. 2.

I know there are going to be people who'll look at our schedule and say we haven't played very many strong teams, but they need to look closer and see who've played the second half of the year."

Alabama defeated four teams ranked in the Top 25 and headed to bowl games in its final six.

GAME STATS AND SCORING

Alabama	7	7	7	7	28
Florida	7	0	7	7	21

STATISTICS

STATISTICS	UA	FLA
First Downs	15	22
Rushing (Att/Yds)	41-132	30-30
Passing (Comp/Atts/Int)	10-18-0	30-49-2
Passing Yards	154	287
Total Offense	286	317
Total Offensive Plays	59	79
Average Gain Per Play	4.85	4.01
Fumbles/Lost	0-0	0-0
Total Turnovers	0	2
Punting (No/Avg)	10-32.6	7-40.0
Punt Returns(No/Yds)	3-31	4-23
Kickoff Returns(No/Yds)	3-14	5-71
Penalties/Yards	11-75	4-30
Time of Possession	28:40	31:20
Third Down Conversions	2-13	4-15
Fourth Down Conversions	1-3	0-0
Sacks/Lost	3-21	3-23

INDIVIDUAL STATISTICS

Rushing (Att-Yds-TD): UA—Lassic 21-121-2;Houston6-22-0;Anderson 2-6-0;Williams 1-2-0;Barker 8-(-4)-0; Palmer 3-(-11)-0
FLA—Rhett 22-59-1; Randolph 1-0-0; Malone 1-(-4)-0; Edge 1-(-12)-0; Matthews 5-(-13)-0
Passing (Comp-Att-Int-Yds-TD): UA—Barker 10-18-0-154-1
UF—Matthews 30-49-0-287-2
Receiving (Rec-Yds-TD): UA—Palmer 5-101-0; C. Brown 1-30-1; Williams 2-16-0; Lee 1-5-0; Anderson 1-2-0
UF—Jackson 9-100-1; Rhett 10-82-1; Randolph 3-31-0; Dean 3-31-0; Keller 2-26-0; Houston 2-10-0; Everett 1-7-0

DEFENSIVE STATISTICS

Tackles (Primary-Assist-Total): UA—Donnelly 6-3-9; W. Brown 7-1-8; Langham 6-2-8; Derrick Oden 5-3-8; Teague 5-1-6; Shade 5-1-6; Nunley 2-4-6
UF—White 7-3-10; Kennedy 6-4-10; Miles 7-2-9; Oliver 7-1-8
Sacks: UA—London 1(-13); Teague 1(-7); Copeland 1(-1)
UF-Miles 1(-10); Johnson 1(-8); Church 1(-5);
Tackles for Losses: UA—Copeland 2 (-9); Swinney 1 (-12); Hall 1 (-3); Nunley 1 (-3); Rogers 1 (-2)-
UF—Miles 1 (-7); Church 1 (-5); Carter 1 (-3); Campbell 1 (-2); Oliver 1 (-2)
Passes Broken Up: UA—London, Donnelly, Tommy Johnson, Langham (1 each)
UF—NONE
Interceptions: UA—Langham 1 (27-yard TD); Rogers 1
UF-NONE
Quarterback Pressures: UA-Nunley 3; London 3; Curry 2; Teague 1; Copland 1

SCORING SUMMARY

First Quarter
UA 0, FLA 7—10:03 Errict Rhett 5-yard pass from Matthews (Davis kick) [11 plays, 77 yards, 4:57]
UA 7, FLA 7—5:07 Derrick Lassic 3-yard run (Michael Proctor kick) [10 plays, 72 yards, 4:56]
Second Quarter
UA 14, FLA 7—4:49 Curtis Brown 30-yard pass (Proctor kick) [5 plays, 42 yards, 2:32]
Third Quarter
UA 21, FLA 7—5:14 Lassic 15-yard run (Proctor kick) [4 plays, 66 yards, 1:33]
UA 21, FLA 14—W. Jackson 4-yard pass from Matthews (Davis kick) [9 plays, 68 yards, 3:53]
Fourth Quarter
UA 21, FLA 21—Rhett 1-yard run (Davis kick) [9 plays, 51 yards, 3:39]
UA 28, FLA 21—Langham 27-yard interception return of Matthews (Proctor kick)

Alabama by the Numbers

Miami	3 3 0 7—13	
Alabama	3 10 14 7— 34	

Sugar Bowl Stats

Alabama 34 Miami 13

First Quarter
Ala—FG Proctor 19
Mia—FG Prewitt 49

Second Quarter
Ala—FG Proctor 23
Ala—S.Williams 2 run (Proctor kick)
Mia—FG Prewitt 42

Third Quarter
Ala—Lassic 1 run (Proctor kick)
Ala—Teague 31 interception return (Proctor kick)

Fourth Quarter
Mia—K.Williams 78 punt return (Prewitt kick)
Ala—Lassic 4 run (Proctor kick)
Attendance— 76,789

	Miami	UA
First downs	16	15
Rushes-yards	18-48	60-267
Passing	278	18
Return Yards	121	139
Comp-Att-Int	24-56-3	4-13-2
Punts	5-41.6	6-44.5
Fumbles-Lost	4-1	0-0
Penalties-Yards	6-37	7-46
Time of Possession ..	23:56	36:04

INDIVIDUALS

MIAMI

Rushing
Player	Att.	Yds.	TD	Long
Bennett	5	28	0	16
L.Jones	3	26	0	13
McGuire	4	1	0	4
Torretta	5	1	0	15
Williams	1	-8	0	0

Passing
Player	A-C-I	Yds	TD	Long
Torretta	56-24-3	278	0	40

Receiving
Player	No.	Yds	TD	Long
C.Jones	3	64	0	40
Thomas	6	52	0	18
Williams	3	49	0	34
Bell	1	34	0	34
Copeland	2	21	0	16
Bennett	4	17	0	7
J.Harris	2	16	0	10
Kirkeide	1	14	0	14
Spencer	1	8	0	8
L.Jones	1	3	0	3

Punting
Player	No.	Yds	Avg	Long
Snyder	5	208	41.6	44

Returns
Player	Punts	Kickoff	Int.
Williams	3-95	7-146	
McNeil			1-0
Greer			1-26

ALABAMA

Rushing
Player	Att.	Yds.	TD	Long
Lassic	28	135	2	25
Lynch	5	39	0	16
Houston	6	23	0	14
Palmer	2	22	0	26
Barker	7	20	0	10
S.Williams	7	18	1	8
Burgdorf	1	6	0	6
Anderson	4	4	0	2

Passing
Player	A-C-I	Yds	TD	Long
Barker	13-4-2	18	0	6

Receiving
Player	No.	Yds	TD	Long
Wimbley	2	11	0	6
Palmer	1	6	0	6
Lassic	1	1	0	1

Punting
Player	No.	Yds	Avg	Long
Diehl	6	267	44.5	57

Returns
Player	Punts	Kickoff	Int.
Palmer	5-52	2-53	
S.Williams		1-20	
Teague			1-31
Shade			1-33
To.Johnson			1-23

DEFENSE

MIAMI
Tackles, assists —Barrow 3-5; Greer 4-4; Smith 7-0; Armstead 5-1; Krein 4-1; T.Harris 5-0; Riley 4-0; Marley 3-1; Bass 2-1; Seigler 3-0; Patrick 3-0; McNeil 3-0; Caesar 3-4; Carey 1-0; Pearson 0-1; Lopez 1-0; Sapp 0-1; Bennett 1-0; Richardson 1-0; Torretta 1-0; Williams 1-0. **Sacks** —Barrow 1, Marley 1. **Fumbles recovered** —None. **Passes intercepted** —McNeil 1, Greer 1. **Passes broken up** —Greer 2, Smith 1, McNeil 1, Sapp 1, White 1.

ALABAMA
Tackles, assists —Gaston 6-1; To.Johnson 6-0; Donnelly 3-1; Teague 3-1; Shade 4-0; Hall 2-1; Oden 3-0; Copeland 2-1; Nunley 2-0; Ausmus 2-0; London 1-1; Bevelle 2-0; Sheils 1-0; Langham 1-0; Turner 1-0; Gregory 1-0; Tony Johnson 1-0; E.Brown 0-1. **Sacks** —Tommy Johnson 1. **Fumbles recovered** —Tommy Johnson 1. **Passes inter-cepted** —Teague 1, Tommy Johnson 1, Shade 1. **Passes broken up** — Tommy Johnson 5, Shade 2, Langham 2, Gaston 1, Teague 1, Hall 1, Turner 1, Curry 1.

ALABAMA SEASON
Results (13-0)

Vanderbilt	Won, 25-8
Southern Miss	Won, 17-10
at Arkansas	Won, 38-11
Louisiana Tech	Won, 13-0
South Carolina	Won, 48-7
at Tulane	Won, 37-0
at Tennessee	Won, 17-10
Mississippi	Won, 31-10
at LSU	Won, 31-11
at Mississippi State	Won, 30-21
Auburn	Won, 17-0
Florida	Won, 28-21
Miami	Won, 34-13

MIAMI SEASON
Results (11-1)

Iowa	Won, 24-7
Florida A&M	Won, 38-0
Arizona	Won, 8-7
Florida St.	Won, 19-16
Penn St.	Won, 17-14
TCU	Won, 45-10
Virginia Tech	Won, 43-23
W.Virginia	Won, 35-23
Temple	Won, 48-0
Syracuse	Won, 16-10
San Diego St.	Won, 63-17
Alabama	Lost, 34-13

Tale of the tape: Alabama vs. Miami

ALABAMA CRIMSON TIDE (12-0-0, 9-0-0 SEC)

COACH: Gene Stallings is 57-51-1 in ten seasons as a head coach. He is 30-6-0 in his three years at Alabama. He is 20-3 against SEC opponents and served as head coach for seven seasons at Texas A&M before embarking on an 18-year career in professional football.

1992 ALABAMA SCHEDULE (12-0)

Sept. 5	Alabama 25, Vanderbilt 8 (JP)
Sept. 12	Alabama 17, USM 10
Sept. 19	Alabama 38, Arkansas 11
Sept. 26	Alabama 13, Louisiana Tech 0
Oct. 3	Alabama 48, South Carolina 7
Oct. 10	Alabama 37, Tulane 0
Oct. 17	Alabama 17, Tennessee 10 (ABC)
Oct. 24	Alabama 31, Ole Miss 10 (JP)
Nov. 7	Alabama 31, LSU 11 (ABC)
Nov. 14	Alabama 30, Miss. State 21 (ESPN)
Nov. 26	Alabama 17, Auburn 0 (ABC)
Dec. 5	Alabama 28, Florida 21 (SEC Championship (ABC)

TYPE OF OFFENSE: Pro "1"
AVG. LINE & TE: 6-3^1/$_2$, 269
AVG. BACKS & RECEIVERS: 5-11^3/$_4$, 198
STARTERS: 2 So., 4 Jr., 5 Sr.

TYPE OF DEFENSE: Multiple
AVG. LINE: 6-5, 275
AVG. LINEBACKERS: 6-1^1/$_4$, 226
AVG. SECONDARY: 6-1, 185
STARTERS: 2 So., 4 Jr., 5 Sr.

MIAMI HURRICANES (11-0-0, 4-0 Big East)

COACH: Dennis Erickson is in his fourth season at the helm of the Miami program. He has compiled a 44-3 record at UM, winning the National Championship in 1989 and 1991. Overall, Erickson is 94-34-1 with stops at Idaho, Wyoming and Washington State.

1992 MIAMI SCHEDULE (11-0)

Sept. 5	Miami 24, Iowa 7 (ABC)
Sept. 19	Miami 38, Florida A&M 0
Sept. 26	Miami 8, Arizona 7
Oct. 3	Miami 19, Florida State 16 (ABC)
Oct. 10	Miami 17, Penn State 14 (ABC)
Oct. 17	Miami 45, TCU 10
Oct. 24	Miami 43, Virginia Tech 23
Oct. 31	Miami 35, West Virginia 23 (ESPN)
Nov. 14	Miami 48, Temple 0 (HC)
Nov. 21	Miami 16, Syracuse 10 (ABC)
Nov. 26	Miami 63, San Diego State 17 (ESPN)

TYPE OF OFFENSE: Pro Passing Attack (One Back)
AVG. LINE & TE: 6-3, 267
AVG. BACKS & RECEIVERS: 6-1, 197
STARTERS: 2 So., 1 Jr., 8 Sr.

TYPE OF DEFENSE: 4-3
AVG. LINE: 6-3^1/$_4$, 268
AVG. LINEBACKERS: 6-2, 238
AVG. SECONDARY: 6-0^1/$_4$, 189
STARTERS: 1 So., 4 Jr., 6 Sr.

1992 STATISTICAL LEADERS

	ALABAMA	MIAMI
SCORING	27.7	32.4
SCORING DEFENSE	9.1	11.5
TOTAL OFFENSE	362.8	436.5
TOTAL DEFENSE	194.2	270.8
RUSHING OFFENSE	208.9	120.5
RUSHING DEFENSE	55.0	101.6
PASSING OFFENSE	153.9	316.0
PASSING DEFENSE	139.2	169.2

INDIVIDUAL LEADERS

PASSING:	Barker (UA) 132-243-1614-7-9	Torretta (UM) 228-402-3060-19-7
RUSHING:	Lassic (UA) 178-905-10	Bennett (UM) 97-421-6
	Anderson (UA) 94-573-7	L. Jones (UM) 85-328-6
	Houston (UA) 103-457-0	Ferguson (UM) 63-305-1
RECEIVING:	Palmer (UA) 24-297-1	Horace Copeland (UM) 47-769-2
	Lee (UA) 21-286-1	Thomas (UM) 47-701-108-0
	Wimbley (UA) 21-248-0	Bell (UM) 43-634-2

1992 University of Alabama final team statistics

OVERALL: 12-0-0   SEC: 9-0   HOME: 6-0   AWAY: 5-0   NEUTRAL: 1-0

ALABAMA FOOTBALL RESULTS

*ALABAMA 25, Vanderbilt 8 (JP)	T—70,123#
ALABAMA 17, Southern Miss 10	B—83,091#
*ALABAMA 38, Arkansas 11	A—55,912#
ALABAMA 13, Louisiana Tech 0	B—77,622
*ALABAMA 48, South Carolina 7 (HC)	T—70,123#
ALABAMA 37, Tulane 0	A—50,240
*ALABAMA 17, Tennessee 10 (ABC)	A—97,388#
*ALABAMA 31, Ole Miss 10 (JP)	T—70,123#
*ALABAMA 31, LSU 11 (ABC)	A—76,813
*ALABAMA 30, Mississippi State 21 (ESPN)	A—41,320#
*ALABAMA 17, Auburn 0 (ABC)	B—83,091#
*ALABAMA 28, Florida 21 (ABC)	N—83,091#

*SEC Game   #Sellout   T—Tuscaloosa   B—Birmingham   A—Away

TEAM STATISTICS

	UM	OPP
TOTAL FIRST DOWNS	241	136
Rushing	142	52
Passing	79	74
Penalty	20	10
NET YARDS RUSHING	2507	660
Yards Rushing	2972	1164
Yards Lost	465	504
Rushing Attempts	588	395
Average gain per rush	4.26	1.67
Average gain per game	208.9	55.0
NET YARDS PASSING	1847	1670
Average Net Per Game	153.9	139.2
Passes Attempted	271	330
Passes Completed	145	164
Had Intercepted	10	22
TOTAL OFFENSE	4354	2330
Average Net Per Game	362.8	194.16
Total Plays	864	725
Average Plays Per Game	72.0	60.4
Average Gain Per Play	5.03	3.21
NUMBER PUNTS/YARDS	64-2444	86-3487
Punting Average	38.2	40.5
Net Punting Average	33.6	36.3
PUNT RETURNS/YARDS	48-373	36-329
Punt Return Average	7.8	9.1
KICXKOFF RETURNS/YARDS	19-317	62-1345
Kickoff Return Average	16.7	21.7
PENALTY/YARDS	77-623	69-577
Average Penalty Yards Per Game	51.9	48.1
FUMBLES/FUMBLES LOST	25-10	34-14
INTERCEPTION RETURNS/YARDS	22-204	10-41
Average Yards Per Return	9.3	4.1
MISCELLANEOUS YARDS	0	0
TOUCHDOWNS	39	12
Rushing	26	5
Passing	8	6
Returns	5	1
POINT AFTER TOUCHDOWNS	38-39	8-8
FIELD GOALS MADE/ATTEMPTS	20-28	7-15
SAFETY	0	1
TWO-POINT CONVERSIONS	0	3-4
TOTAL POINTS	332	109
Average Per Game	27.7	9.1

RUSHING

Player	G	ATT	GAIN	LOSS	NET	AVG	TD	AVG/GM	LONG
Lassic	12	178	980	75	905	5.1	10	75.4	42
Anderson	12	94	600	27	573	6.1	7	47.8	57
Houston	12	103	465	8	457	4.4	0	38.1	45
Palmer	9	26	191	27	164	6.3	0	18.2	39
Williams	12	64	337	38	299	4.5	8	24.9	26
Lynch	12	25	92	0	92	3.7	0	7.7	12
Burgdorf	5	11	43	10	33	3.3	0	7.2	18
Lee	11	3	43	2	41	13.7	0	3.7	24
Harris	11	3	43	2	41	13.7	0	3.7	24
Wimbley	12	4	21	2	19	4.8	0	1.6	9
Key	1	1	0	4	−4	−4.0	0	−4.0	—
Barker	12	64	153	247	−94	−1.5	0	−8.2	33

PASSING

Player	G	ATT	CMP	PCT	INT	YDS	TD	LONG	SACKS
Barker	12	243	132	.543	9	1614	7	46	31/(−242)
Burgdorf	5	23	12	.522	1	160	0	51	1/(−1)
Diehl	12	1	1	1.000	0	73	1	73	0/0
Key	1	0	0	.000	0	0	0	0	1/(−4)
Palmer	9	3	0	.000	0	0	0	0	0/0
Williams	12	1	0	.000	0	0	0	0	0/0

RECEIVING

Player	G	REC	YDS	TD	AVG	YDS/GM	LONG
Palmer	9	24	297	1	12.4	33.0	39
Lee	11	21	286	1	13.6	26.0	46
Wimbley	12	21	248	0	11.8	20.7	24
C. Brown	12	20	327	2	16.4	27.3	30
Anderson	12	14	147	1	10.5	12.3	36
Lassic	12	14	129	1	9.2	10.8	29
Williams	12	9	120	0	13.3	10.0	24
Busky	12	8	81	1	10.1	6.8	26
Houston	12	6	26	0	4.3	2.2	9
Swinney	12	4	48	0	12.0	4.0	19
Lynch	12	4	65	0	21.7	5.4	51
Tommy Johnson	12	1	73	1	73.0	6.1	73

FIELD GOALS

Player	G	FGM	FGA	PCT	LONG
Michael Proctor	12	19	27	.704	47
Hamp Greene	3	1	1	1.000	24

FIELD GOAL BREAKDOWN

Player	0-19	20-29	30-39	40-49	50+
Michael Proctor	0-0	7-7	6-10	6-9	0-1
Hamp Greene	0-0	1-1	0-0	0-0	0-0

PUNTING

Player	G	NO.	YDS	AVG	LONG
Bryne Diehl	12	64	2444	38.2	58

KICKOFF RETURNS

Player	G	NO	YDS	AVG	TD	AVG/GM	LONG
David Palmer	9	6	145	24.2	0	16.1	32
Chris Anderson	12	5	103	20.6	0	8.6	25
Kevin Lee	11	2	36	18.0	0	3.3	19
Sherman Williams	12	2	30	15.0	0	2.5	16
Craig Harris	11	2	14	7.0	0	1.3	

PUNT RETURNS

Player	G	NO	YDS	AVG	TD	AVG/GM	LONG
Antonio Langham	12	1	24	24.0	1	2.0	24
David Palmer	9	28	236	8.4	1	26.2	63
Chris Anderson	12	16	93	5.8	0	7.8	21

1992 Alabama Defensive Statistics

PLAYER	G	T	TFL	SACKS	QBP	INT/ YDS	PBU	FC	FR	BLKD KICKS
Lemanski Hall, OLB	12	70	8-19	5-32	11		2		3	
Michael Rogers, ILB	12	68	10-20	1-5		2-36	1			
John Copeland, DE	12	65	11-25	10.5/45	22		5	3	2	
Derrick Oden, ILB	12	65	6-13	2-11	2		1	1		
Antonio London, OLB	12	61	4-13	4-41	10		4	4		1 (FG)
Sam Shade, SS	12	60	1-5			2-16	4		2	
Chris Donnelly, FS	12	47				3-21	6			
George Teague, CB	12	42	1-1	1-7	1	6-(0)	7	2	1	1 (P)
Antonio Langham, CB	12	41		1-6		6-114	4			1 (P)
Eric Curry, DE	12	40	7-24	10.5/59	27		1	2		
Tommy Johnson, CB	12	34			1	2-17	1	1	1	
James Gregory, NT	10	32	3-12	2-10	4			1		
Jeremy Nunley, DE	10	25	3-10	4-37	7			1		
Will Brown, OLB	12	25	2-6	2-17	3					
Mario Morris, ILB	12	22					1			
Willie Gaston, CB	21					1-0	3			
John Walters, ILB	12	16							1	
Eric Turner, SS	10	14					1			
Dameian Jeffries, DE	9	11	1-2	3-17	1				1	
Victor Lockett, OLB	10	11	1-1	2-11	1					
Shannon Brown, NT	9	8	2-3	2-12						
Matthew Pine, SN/TE	12	7					1			
Bryan Thornton, DE	5	6	1-6						1	
Danny Davis, SS	9	6								
Mickey Conn, CB	6	6								
Tony Johnson, TE	12	5								
Michael Ausmus, SS	10	5	1-1							
Willis Bevelle, OLB	12	4							1	
Andre Royal, ILB	4	4	1-1						1	
Elverett Brown, NT	6	4	101				1			
Kris Mangum, TE	10	3								
Jeff Foshee, ILB	12	3								
Jason Milner, DE	4	3								
Craig Harris, FB	11	3								
Dabo Swinney, SE	12	3	1-12							
Bryne Diehl, P	12	2						1		
Chris Anderson, RB	12	1								
Jeff Torrence, ILB	12	1								
Hamp Greene, PK	3	1								
Jeff Wall, CB	12	1								
Roman Colburn, FL	6	1								
Myron Pope, TE	10	1								
Sherman Williams, RB	12	1								
Tarrant Lynch, FB	12	1								
Derrick Lassic, RB	12	1								

G-games, T-tackles TFL-tackles for loss QBP-quarterback pressures
INT-interceptions PBU-passes broken up FC-fumbles caused
FR-fumbles recovered

Game-by-Game Leaders

Opponent	Tackles
VANDERBILT	
John Copeland	12
Derrick Oden	12
Antonio London	11
James Gregory	7
For Losses	
Lemanski Hall	2-4
John Copeland	2-2
Eight with one each	
SOUTHERN MISS	
Lemanski Hall	8
Antonio London	7
Eric Curry	6
For Losses	
Lemanski Hall	2-6
Five with one each	
ARKANSAS	
Lemanski Hall	7
Michael Rogers	6
George Teague	4
For Losses	
Dameian Jeffries	2-12
Michael Rogers	2-3
Jeremy Nunley	1-5
LOUISIANA TECH	
Michael Rogers	9
Antonio London	7
Copeland/Hall	6
For Losses	
John Copeland	2-6
Jeremy Nunley	2-7
Three with one each	
SOUTH CAROLINA	
Victor Lockett	5
Will Brown	5
Mario Morris	5
Seven with four each	
For Losses	
Six with one each	
TULANE	
Derrick Oden	8
Sam Shade	6
Willie Gaston	5
For Losses	
Eric Curry	3-15
Dameian Jeffries	2-6
Two with one each	
TENNESSEE	
Michael Rogers	8
George Teague	5
Three with four each	
For Losses	
Eric Curry	2-3
Three with one each	
OLE MISS	
Derrick Oden	9
Sam Shade	6
Three with five each	
For Losses	
John Copeland	2-3
Michael Rogers	1-4
LSU	
Michael Rogers	11
Lemanski Hall	10
Antonio London	8
For Losses	
John Copeland	3-10
MISSISSIPPI STATE	
Lemanski Hall	15
Sam Shade	10
Tommy Johnson	9
Two with eight each	
For Losses	
Four with one each	
AUBURN	
John Copeland	8
Eric Curry	7
Chris Donnelly	7
Sam Shade	7
For Losses	
Two with one each	
FLORIDA	
Chris Donnelly	9
Will Brown	8
Antonio Langham	8
Derrick Oden	8
For Losses	
John Copeland	2-9
Four with one each	

1992 University of Alabama Football Superlatives

(Through 12 Games)

LONGEST RUN FROM SCRIMMAGE: 57 by Chris Anderson vs. Tulane
LONGEST PASS PLAY: 73 by Bryne Diehl to Tommy Johnson vs. USM (TD)
LONGEST KICKOFF RETURN: 32 by David Palmer vs. Tulane
LONGEST PUNT RETURN: 63 by·David Palmer vs. Louisiana Tech (TD)
LONGEST FIELD GOAL: 47 by Michael Proctor vs. Auburn
LONGEST PUNT: 58 by Bryne Diehl vs. Tennessee
LONGEST INTERCEPTION RETURN: 61 by Antonio Langham vs. Auburn (TD)
LONGEST SCORING DRIVE (Yards): 99 yards vs. Arkansas
MOST RUSHING ATTEMPTS: 33 by Derrick Lassic vs. Tennessee (142 yards)
MOST YARDS GAINED RUSHING: 188 yards by Derrick Lassic vs. Tulane (20 atts.)
MOST PASSING ATTEMPTS: 39 by Jay Barker vs. Ole Miss (25 comp.)
MOST PASSES COMPLETED: 25 by Jay Barker vs. Ole Miss (39 att.)
MOST YARDS GAINED PASSING: 285 by Jay Barker vs. Ole Miss (25-of-39)
MOST PASS RECEPTIONS: 8 by Kevin Lee vs. Ole Miss (82 yards)
MOST YARDS GAINED RECEIVING: 101 yards by David Palmer vs. Florida (5 receptions)
MOST YARDS TOTAL OFFENSE: 280 by Jay Barker vs. Ole Miss (285 pass, -5 rush)
MOST ALL-PURPOSE YARDS: 213 by Chris Anderson vs. LSU (149 rush, 6 rec., 58 KOR)
MOST POINTS SCORED: 13 by Michael Proctor vs. Vandy (4 FG, 1 PAT)

HIGH AND LOW TIDES

OFFENSE	BEST	WORST
POINTS SCORED	48 vs. South Carolina	13 vs. Louisiana Tech
FIRST DOWNS	29 vs. South Carolina	13 vs. Louisiana Tech
Rushing	19 vs. S. Carolina/Tulane/Tennessee	6 vs. La. Tech/Ole Miss
Passing	12 vs. Ole Miss	2 vs. Tennessee
Penalty	4 vs. Ole Miss	0 vs. LSU
RUSHING ATTEMPTS	66 vs. Tennessee	34 vs. Vanderbilt
NET YARDS RUSHING	435 vs. Tulane	67 vs. Louisiana Tech
NET YARDS PASSING	285 vs. Ole Miss	54 vs. Tennessee
Passes Attempted	39 vs. Ole Miss	11 vs. Tennessee
Passes Completed	25 vs. Ole Miss	5 vs. Tennessee/Auburn
Had Intercepted	0 vs. Tulane/Tennessee/LSU/Florida	2 vs. vs. MSU/Auburn
OFFENSIVE PLAYS	81 vs. Arkansas	61 vs. Vanderbilt
TOTAL YARDS	573 vs. Tulane	167 vs. Louisiana Tech
Avg. Gain Per Play	7.96 vs. Tulane	2.49 vs. Louisiana Tech
RETURN YARDS	92 vs. Auburn	-1 vs. LSU
FUMBLES	0 vs. Louisiana Tech/Florida	6 vs. USM
FUMBLES LOST	0 vs. La. Tech/Ole Miss/LSU/Florida	3 vs. Arkansas
TOTAL TURNOVERS	0 vs. LSU/Florida	4 vs. Arkansas
PENALTIES	2 vs. Miss. St.	11 vs. FLorida
YARDS PENALIZED	10 vs. Miss. St.	95 vs. Arkansas
PUNTS	3 vs. Vanderbilt	10 vs. Florida
PUNTING AVERAGE	46.8 vs. Tulane	32.6 vs. Florida

DEFENSE	BEST	WORST
POINTS ALLOWED	0 vs. La.Tech/Tulane/Auburn	21 vs. Miss. St./Florida
FIRST DOWNS	3 vs. USM	18 vs. Miss. St.
Rushing	2 vs. USM/La. Tech	12 vs. Vanderbilt
Passing	0 vs. USM	13 vs. LSU
Penalty	0 vs. 5 times; last vs. MSU	2 vs. Arkansas/Tulane/Ole Miss
RUSHING ATTEMPTS	25 vs. Arkansas	61 vs. Vanderbilt
NET YARDS RUSHING	-8 vs. Louisiana Tech	138 vs. Vanderbilt
NET YARDS PASSING	26 vs. USM	287 vs. Florida
TOTAL OFFENSIVE PLAYS	46 vs. USM	79 vs. Florida
TOTAL YARDS	54 vs. USM	317 vs. Florida
Avg. Gain Per Play	0.79 vs. Louisiana Tech	4.4 vs. Miss. St.
FUMBLES	7 vs. South Carolina	0 vs. Ole Miss/Florida
FUMBLES RECOVERED	3 vs. Vandy/Arkansas	0 vs. Tulane/Tennessee/Florida
PASSES INTERCEPTED	4 vs. Tulane	0 vs. La. Tech/S. Carolina/Tenn.
TOTAL TURNOVERS	5 vs. Tulane	1 vs. La. Tech/Tennessee

School Records and Honors for the 1992 Season

TEAM RECORDS

VICTORIES
12
(Ties record from 1979)

MOST PENALTIES IN A SEASON
77
(Old record 76 in 1986)

INDIVIDUAL RECORDS

SCORING BY A FRESHMAN (SEASON)
94 by Michael Proctor (19 FG, 37 PAT)
(Old record 82 by Van Tiffin, 1983)

INTs RETURNED FOR TD (SEASON CAREER)
2 by Antonio Langham
(Ties season record held by Hootie Ingram and Bobby Johns, ties career record held by Ingram, Johns and Steve Higginbotham)

MOST BLOCKED KICKS RECOVERED FOR TDs IN A GAME
1 (punt) by Antonio Langham vs. Miss. State
(Old record 1 by three; last being Antonio Langham, Vanderbilt 1990)

TDs BY A DEFENSIVE PLAYER (SEASON)
3 Antonio Langham

MOST PUNTS RETURNED FOR TD (CAREER)
4 by David Palmer (3 in 1991, 1 in 1992)

1992 HONORS WON

ALL-AMERICA
FIRST TEAM
Eric Curry (AP, UPI, Walter Camp, Kodak-Coaches)
John Copeland (AP, Walter Camp, Football Writers, Kodak-Coaches, *Football News*)
SECOND TEAM
George Teague (UPI)
THIRD TEAM
Antonio Langham (AP)
HONORABLE MENTION
John Copeland (UPI)
Tobie Sheils (UPI)

CHEVROLET "DEFENSIVE PLAYER OF THE YEAR"
Eric Curry

PIGSKIN CLUB OF WASHINGTON, D.C. "LINEMAN OF THE YEAR"
Eric Curry

UPI "LINEMAN OF THE YEAR"
Eric Curry

FINALIST—FOOTBALL NEWS "DEFENSIVE PLAYER OF THE YEAR"
John Copeland

PIGSKIN CLUB OF WASHINGTON, D.C. "COACH OF THE YEAR"
Coach Gene Stallings

FINALIST FOOTBALL NEWS "COACH OF THE YEAR"
Coach Gene Stallings

BIRMINGHAM NEWS "SEC COACH OF THE YEAR"
Coach Gene Stallings

LOMBARDI AWARD FINALIST
Eric Curry

PAUL BRYANT AWARD (COACH OF THE YEAR—FOOTBALL WRITERS ASSOCIATION OF AMERICA)
Coach Gene Stallings

ALL-SEC
FIRST TEAM
John Copeland (AP, Coaches, *Birmingham News, Football News*)
Eric Curry (AP, Coaches, *Birmingham News, Football News*)
Lemanski Hall (Coaches, *Birmingham News*)
Antonio Langham (AP, Coaches, *Birmingham News*)
Derrick Lassic (*Birmingham News*)
Antonio London (Coaches, *Football News*)
Derrick Oden (Coaches)
Tobie Sheils (AP, Coaches, *Birmingham News, Football News*)
George Teague (AP, Coaches, *Birmingham News, Football News*)
SECOND TEAM
Lemanski Hall (AP)
Derrick Lassic (AP, Coaches)
Michael Proctor (AP)
George Wilson (Coaches)

SEC "PLAYER OF THE WEEK"
Michael Proctor (offensive) vs. Vanderbilt
John Copeland (defensive) vs. Tennessee
Jay Barker (offensive) vs. Ole Miss
Chris Anderson (offensive) vs. LSU
George Teague (defensive) vs. Mississippi State

ABC CHEVROLET "PLAYER OF THE GAME"
Derrick Lassic vs. Tennessee
Chris Anderson vs. LSU
Antonio Langham vs. Auburn
Derrick Lassic vs. Florida (SEC Championship)

ESPN "PLAYER OF THE GAME"
George Teague vs. Mississippi State

JEFFERSON PILOT "PLAYER OF THE GAME"
Michael Proctor vs. Vanderbilt
Jay Barker vs. Ole Miss

SEC CHAMPIONSHIP MVP
Antonio Langham

PRE-SEASON ALL-SEC
Tobie Sheils
David Palmer
John Copeland
Eric Curry
Antonio London
George Teague

COLLEGE & PRO FOOTBALL WEEKLY "DEFENSIVE PLAYER OF THE WEEK"
John Copeland vs. Tennessee

SPORTING NEWS "DEFENSIVE PLAYER OF THE WEEK"
George Teague vs. Mississippi State

JAPAN BOWL
John Copeland
Eric Curry

HULA BOWL
Eric Curry

EAST-WEST SHRINE GAME
John Copeland

SENIOR BOWL
John Copeland
Eric Curry
Martin Houston
Derrick Lassic
Antonio London
Derrick Oden
George Teague
Prince Wimbley

1992 Alabama Crimson Tide Alphabetical Roster

NO.	NAME, POS	CLASS	HT	WT	EXP	HOMETOWN
89*	Jason Abrams, TE	Jr.	6-4	230	SQ	Demopolis
12*	J.J. Adams, P	So.	6-1	165	SQ	Katy, TX
33	Chris Anderson, RB	Jr.	5-9	178	2VL	Huntsville
26	Michael Ausmus, RCB	Fr.	5-9	170	SQ	Mobile
62	William Barger, RG	Jr.	6-3	270	2VL	Birmingham
7	Jay Barker, QB	So.	6-3	209	1VL	Trussville
66	Tim Barnett, C	Fr.	6-5	263	SQ	Bear Creek
64	Maurice Belser, OL	Fr.	6-2	285	HS	Cordova
6	Willis Bevelle, FL	Sr.	6-1	180	2VL	Bessemer
44	Darrell Blackburn, LB	Fr.	6-4	220	HS	Huntsville
97	Vann Bodden, RDE	Fr.	6-4	235	SQ	Moss Point, MS
48	Jay Brannen, OLB	So.	6-1	218	SQ	Gainesville, FL
85	Curtis Brown, SE	So.	6-3	185	1VL	John's Island, SC
76	Elverett Brown, NT	So.	6-4	261	1VL	Montgomery
82	Rick Brown, FL	So.	6-0	175	1VL	Ft. Worth, TX
93	Shannon Brown, LDE	Fr.	6-5	263	SQ	Millbrook
14	Brian Burgdorf, QB	Fr.	6-1	175	SQ	Cedartown, GA
41*	Anthony Burrouoghs, FB	Fr.	5-11	201	SQ	Rogersville
83	Steve Busky, TE	Sr.	6-6	233	2VL	Suitland, MD
38	Mike Campbell, SE	Sr.	6-0	185	1VL	Pinson
71	John Causey, OL	Fr.	6-3	260	HS	Hayneville
59	John Clay, LG	Jr.	6-2	265	2VL	Nashville, TN
84	Roman Colburn, FL	So.	6-0	175	SQ	Ft. Payne
18	Lorenzo Cole, FL	Jr.	5-10	175	1VL	Florence
48	Steve Cole, PK	Jr.	5-9	162	1VL	Fayetteville, GA
40	Mickey Conn, LCB	So.	5-10	175	SQ	Snellville, GA
94	John Copeland, LDE	Sr.	6-3	261	1VL	Lanett
80	Eric Curry, RDE	Sr.	6-7	255	2VL	Thomasville, GA
27	Danny Davis, SS	So.	6-1	205	SQ	Memphis, TN
67	Dennis Deason, C	Jr.	6-1	270	TR	Vestavia
18*	Willie Dickerson, RCB	So.	5-11	190	SQ	Ozark
12	Bryne Diehl, P	So.	6-3	202	SQ	Oakman
72	Pete DiMario, OL	Fr.	6-5	270	HS	Tuscaloosa
21	Chris Donnelly, SS	Jr.	6-0	180	SQ	Germantown, TN
50*	Don Dover, C	Sr.	6-2	254	SQ	Birmingham
56*	Mike Favors, RG	Fr.	6-2	272	SQ	Mobile
50*	Howie Fell, ILB	Fr.	6-1	225	SQ	Birmingham
15	Donnie Finkley, SE	Sr.	5-10	175	2VL	Mobile
65	Napoleon Folks, RG	So.	6-3	288	SQ	Montgomery
49	Jeff Foshee, ILB	So.	5-9	204	1VL	Millbrook
57	Lamont Floyd, LB	Fr.	6-2	240	HS	Orange Park, FL
22	Willie Gaston, DB	So.	5-11	180	HS	Mobile
54	Chad Gladden, C	So.	6-3	254	1VL	Centre
81	Hamp Greene, PK	Sr.	5-11	185	1VL	Montgomery
98	James Gregory, NT	Jr.	6-4	283	2VL	St. Louis, MO
11	Lemanski Hall, OLB	Jr.	6-1	220	2VL	Valley
63	Matt Hammond, LT	Jr.	6-3	266	2VL	Fort Payne
30	Craig Harris, FB	Sr.	5-11	205	3VL	Panama City, FL
60	Joey Harville, LT	So.	6-5	276	1VL	Moulton
9	Alvin Hope, RCB	Sr.	5-10	187	1VL	Mobile
35	Martin Houston, FB	Sr.	5-10	235	3VL	Centre
75	Johnny Howard, SN	Sr.	6-4	270	3VL	Bessemer
98*	John Hutt, ILB	So.	6-0	213	SQ	Tuscaloosa
8*	Jason Jack, QB	So.	6-1	180	SQ	Oxford
3	Ray Jack, PK	Fr.	6-3	215	SQ	Tuscaloosa
91	Dameian Jeffries, RDE	So.	6-4	256	1VL	Sylacauga
10	Tommy Johnson, RCB	So.	5-10	175	1VL	Niceville. FL
5	Tony Johnson, TE	Fr.	6-4	240	SQ	Como, MS
41	Alex Jordan, SS	Jr.	6-0	188	1VL	Hueytown
19	Chad Key, QB	Fr.	6-4	201	SQ	Parrish
86	Will Knowlton, OLB	Fr.	6-3	206	Sq	Fayette
3*	Alex LaBelleman, PK	Fr.	6-0	180	SQ	Maitland, FL
43	Antonio Langham, LCB	Jr.	6-1	170	2VL	Town Creek
25	Derrick Lassic, RB	Sr.	5-11	186	3VL	Haverstraw, NY
64	Kirk Lawson, RT	So.	6-5	270	SQ	Florence
37	Kevin Lee, SE	Jr.	6-1	186	2VL	Mobile
99	Victor Lockett, ILB	Jr.	6-0	243	2VL	Mobile
55	Antonio London, OLB	Sr.	6-3	228	3VL	Tullahoma, TN
47	Jackson Lowery, SS	So.	6-2	195	SQ	Huntsville
45	Tarrant Lynch, FB	So.	6-0	224	1VL	Town Creek
76	Jeff McCullough, C	Fr.	6-4	255	SQ	Oneonta
43	Steve McLaughlin, RB	Fr.	5-10	165	SQ	Garden City, NY
89	Kris Mangum, TE	Fr.	6-5	245	HS	Magee, MS
74	Kareem McNeal, RT	Fr.	6-5	287	SQ	Tuskegee
92	Jason Milner, RDE	So.	6-4	260	SQ	Broken Arrow, OK
95	Kelvin Moore, LB	Fr.	6-3	240	HS	Daphne
58	Mario Morris, ILB	So.	6-0	220	1VL	Decatur
2*	Stan Moss, P	Sr.	6-3	192	SQ	Brent
67*	Scott Mullenix, OL	Jr.	6-3	270	TR	Jacksonville, FL
73	Jeremy Nunley, LDE	Jr.	6-5	247	2VL	Winchester, TN
56	Derrick Oden, ILB	Sr.	6-0	225	3VL	Tuscaloosa
2	David Palmer, FL	So.	5-9	170	1VL	Birmingham
77	Roosevelt Patterson, RT	Jr.	6-4	290	1VL	Mobile
79	Jeremy Pennington, OL	Fr.	6-3	270	HS	Vernon
77*	John Phillips, NT	Sr.	6-1	265	SQ	Atlanta, GA
87	Matthew Pine, SN	Jr.	6-3	221	2VL	Gadsden
42	Myron Pope, OLB	Jr.	6-3	217	SQ	Sweetwater
20*	Jason Porch, P	Fr.	6-1	180	SQ	Scottsboro
78	Ozell Powell, DL	Fr.	6-5	245	HS	Greenville
71*	Bart Pritchett, NT	Sr.	6-1	249	SQ	Mobile
3	Michael Proctor, PK	Fr.	5-11	175	HS	Pelham
52	Michael Rogers, ILB	So.	6-1	220	1VL	Luverne
70	Rory Segrest, RT	Fr.	6-5	265	SQ	Waycross, GA
41*	James Shackelford, FS	So.	5-11	170	SQ	Plant City, FL
31	Sam Shade, SS	So.	6-1	190	1VL	Birmingham
61	Tobie Sheils, C	Jr.	6-3	250	2VL	Fairhope
69	Jon Stevenson, RG	So.	6-2	273	1VL	Memphis, TN
88	Dabo Swinney, SE	Sr.	6-1	180	2VL	Pelham
46	John Tanks, LB	Fr.	6-4	215	HS	Butler
13	George Teague, FS	Sr.	6-2	187	3VL	Montgomery
96	Bryan Thornton, LDE	Fr.	6-7	280	SQ	Mobile
53	Jeff Torrence, ILB	Fr.	6-1	215	SQ	Atmore
86*	DeLan Trimble, OLB	So.	6-1	230	SQ	Cullman
92*	James Tuley, PK	Jr.	5-10	200	SQ	Montgomery
39	Eric Turner, FB	Fr.	6-1	200	HS	Ft.Payne
59*	Thad Turnipseed, OLB	So.	6-0	201	SQ	Montgomery
16	Jeff Wall, H	Sr.	5-7	160	3VL	Birmingham
90	John Walters, LB	Fr.	6-2	225	HS	Dallas, TX
1	Marcell West, WR	Fr.	5-11	175	HS	Niceville, FL
4	Matt Wethington, PK	So.	5-11	170	1VL	Titusville, FL
40*	Tab Whisenhunt, ILB	Sr.	6-2	220	SQ	Bessemen
51	Laron White, DL	Fr.	6-2	260	HS	Courtland
20	Sherman Williams, RB	So.	5-10	190	1VL	Mobile
68	George Wilson, LG	Sr.	6-2	263	2VL	Bessemer
32	Prince Wimbley, FL	Sr.	5-10	174	3VL	Miami, FL
29	Rock Woody, LCB	So.	5-10	180	1VL	Springville

*Duplicate Number

Final Season Review

Final Season Review

August 23, 1992

Coming off an 11-1 season and a No. 5 ranking, the Tide is ranked 9th in the AP pre-season poll. Miami is ranked first, Washington second, Notre Dame third, Florida fourth, Florida State fifth. Alabama receives one first place vote.

Sept. 5

With do-everything star David Palmer suspended by coach Gene Stallings because of a June 26 DUI arrest, Alabama faces heavy-underdog Vanderbilt at Tuscaloosa. The Tide scores only one offensive TD, but the defense sets the tenor of the season, causing five turnovers in the first half. The Tide survives 25-8. After the game, Palmer is arrested again for DUI, his second offense in 11 weeks.

Sept. 7

The Tide rises to No. 8 in first regular season AP poll.

Sept. 12

Southern Miss comes calling on the Tide at Legion Field, and Bama defense presents its calling

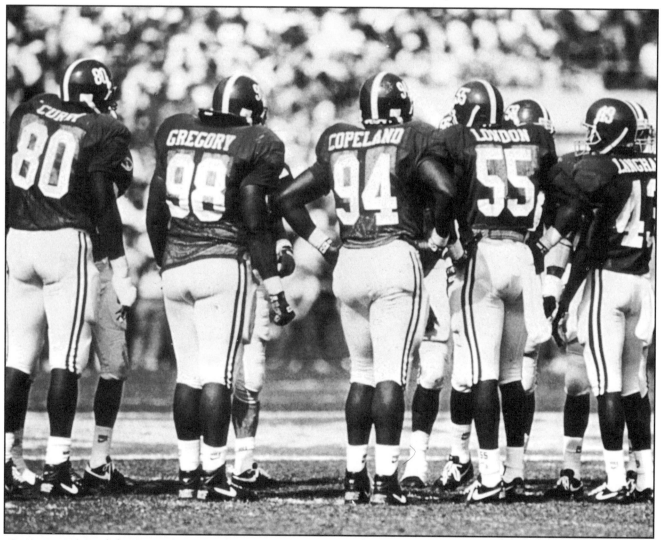

The nation's best defense

National coach of the year Gene Stallings makes his point on the sideline

card, throwing the Golden Eagles for three straight losses on first three plays. USM offense is squelched, netting 28 yards rushing and 26 passing and only three first downs. But two Tide turnovers lead to a 10-7 deficit, the only Bama score coming early on punter Bryne Diehl's 73 yard pass to defensive back Tommy Johnson. Chris Anderson's TD with 10:19 left brings Tide in, but not easily, 17-10.

Sept. 18

Tide's lackluster offensive showing apparently concerns pollsters; Bama slips to No. 9. Alabama still garners its one first place vote.

Sept. 19

Tide hits road to Little Rock to meet SEC new-comer Arkansas. Surprise guests are future president Clinton and Tide offense (467 total yards). Jay Barker hits 14 of 17 passes for 192 yards and three TDs, Derrick Lassic rushes for 118 yards and the Tide builds a 28-0 half-time score before cruising home 38-11.

Sept. 21

Pollsters impressed by points. Tide jumps two notches to No. 7. Miami still No. 1.

Sept. 26

The Deuce is loose! And it's a good thing, as Alabama needs every bit of spark to beat a stubborn Louisiana Tech team at Legion Field, 13-0. The reinstated Palmer brings back a punt 63 yards with 8:18 left to support two Michael Proctor field goals. The Tide defense is usual stingy self, hanging minus eight yards rushing on Tech, and handing the Bulldogs their first shutout in 45 games.

Sept. 28

Shutout doesn't impress AP as Tide falls to No. 9; Washington is new No. 1 team as Miami squeaks by Arizona 8-7.

Oct. 3

Tide lights up a damp, dreary homecoming with 48-7 thrashing of South Carolina. A 21-point first period sets tone as Tide runs wild behind Anderson (120 yards) and Lassic (100 yards). Palmer has his best outing with 118 all-purpose yards and Tide defense holds Gamecocks to 43 yards rushing, the fourth sub-100 yard effort of the season.

Oct. 5

Points count. Tide shoots to No. 6. Washington still first despite Hurricanes' win over FSU.

Oct. 10

Tide travels to Louisiana Superdome as a 27-point favorite to Tulane. Held to two Proctor field goals in the first half, the Tide gets rolling behind Lassic (188 yards) and Anderson (84 yards, 2 TDs). In all, Tide amasses 435 rushing yards. The defense holds the

Quarterback Jay Barker worked hard all season to improve

Stallings scratches his head during pre-season practice trying to put the pieces together for a championship run

Green Wave to 58 yards rushing and grabs five turnovers on way to 37-0 win. The lone Tide No. 1 voter in the AP poll is revealed— it's Tucson (Ariz.) Citizen sportswriter Corky Simpson.

Oct. 12

Tide skips two spots to No. 4. Washington maintains a one-point edge over Miami. Tennessee falls to No. 13 after upset loss to Arkansas, taking some of the luster off the upcoming Third Saturday in October.

Oct. 17

Alabama is one-point favorite heading to Knoxville for Third Saturday meeting with 13th-ranked Vols. Tide mounts a 17-3 half-time lead and then holds on for 17-10 win, the seventh straight Alabama win in the series. A crowd of 97,388 sees Tide defense sack Heath Shuler five times, and strangle Vol runners for 78 yards. The offense contributes Lassic's 142 yards (his third straight 100-yard game), and 301 total yards on the ground. The outcome isn't a certainty until late. Martin Houston fumbles to Tennessee at the Tide 48 with 1:33 left, but the defense rises to the occasion. Michael Rogers tips a Shuler pass and Chris Don-

nelly collects it to preserve the win.

Oct. 19

Tide still at No. 4, but gains ground on No. 3 Michigan. Washington and Miami are tied for first. Tide takes week off, gets ready for Ole Miss.

Oct. 24

Improved Rebels invade Tuscaloosa as 17-point underdogs and dare Tide to throw the ball. Barker responds with career day, hitting 25 of 39 passes for 285 yards. Palmer has his 10th 100-yard all-purpose game in his career as Tide wins 31-10.

Oct. 26

Poll-watching: Miami leads Washington by one point; Alabama at No. 4 gets only other first place vote—presumably, Corky Simpson's. Tide has week off.

Nov. 7

Tide clinches at least a tie for SEC West title with 31-11 win at LSU. Lassic leaves game with bruised shoulder, but Tide grounds out 301 rushing yards behind Anderson (149 yards) and Sherman Williams

(69). Defense allows only 22 yards rushing, racks up six sacks, creates four turnovers, including three interceptions—two by George Teague.

Nov. 9

Miami stays first, but Tide rises to No. 2, as Washington falls to Arizona, and Tide fans start having sweet dreams.

Nov. 14

Tide travels to Starkville for tussle with Mississippi State. Bama clinches SEC West with 30-21 win. The Bulldogs rally from 20-3 deficit to lead 21-20 in the fourth quarter. As Tide fans start to think the unthinkable, Barker completes a third down pass to Prince Wimbley to keep a drive alive. Proctor's 26 yard field goal with 8:10 left puts Tide ahead for good. Teague's two picks and Antonio Langham's blocked punt for a TD are defensive highlights.

Nov. 16

'Canes still 1, Tide still 2. Bama has week off, prepares for Thanksgiving date with Auburn.

Nov. 23

No change in polls, but FSU climbs back in pic-

Assistant head coach Mal Moore took criticism, but in the end helped engineer another national championship.

ture at No. 3. Iron Bowl talk punctuated by Pat Dye resignation on eve of game.

Nov. 26

Bama wins an Iron Bowl awash with emotion 17-0. Tide and Tigers struggle through scoreless first half, but Tide, 15{-point favorite, dominates defensively. Crimsons finally break through with Langham's 61-yard interception return. It is first-ever shutout of a Dye team, and in his last game. Houston leads Tide runners with 68 yards. Defense records five sacks, three takeaways, one separated shoulder (Stan White's) and limits Tigers to eight first downs and 20 yards rushing.

Nov. 30

'Canes stay on top, Tide stays second. Florida's Gators last obstacle to Sugar Bowl slot, National Championship shot.

Dec. 5

At Legion Field, the SEC makes history with its championship game. Western champ Alabama, a 10-point favorite, and Florida, the Eastern champ, battle for the Sugar Bowl berth, and for the Tide, a shot at the national title. Alabama grabs momentum early, building a 21-7 lead. But Gators' Shane Matthews brings Florida back to 21-21 fourth quarter tie. With 3:16 left and following a Bama punt, the momentum now belongs to the Gators. But Langham picks off Matthews on the sideline and races 27 sweet yards for the winning score.

Dec. 7

Final regular season poll: Miami 1, Alabama 2.

Dec. 24

Tide starting linebacker Michael Rogers is injured in a Christmas Eve wreck and will miss the Sugar Bowl.

Jan. 1

Amid the hype, the trash talk, the unbeaten streaks, and the traditions is a football game. Miami, an 8{ point favorite, simply is outcoached and out-played by the Tide 34-13. The game is microcosm of the season. ``One-dimensional'' Tide piles up 267 yards on ground, led by game MVP Lassic's 135 yards. Palmer has a punt return to set up a Proctor field goal. The defense, brilliantly prepared by Bill Oliver and perfectly executed by the nation's best unit, confuses Heisman Trophy winner Gino Torretta to a 24 of 56, three-interception performance, and smothers the 'Cane ground game to 48 yards. Johnson, Sam Shade and Teague pick off Torretta, with Teague going for a score. The Play of Which Legends Are Made: Torretta connects with Lamar Thomas for what seems to be a sure Miami score. But Teague tracks down Thomas 82 yards later and rips the ball away. Even with an open field and a track man hauling the ball, the defense didn't give up. Thomas and Miami were left—finally—speechless.

Jan. 2

The AP poll makes it official: Alabama is the National Champion. Corky's vote is now just one of 62.

Epilogue

by Clyde Bolton

NEW ORLEANS—What's left for the critics to say? That Alabama is the worst team they ever saw that went 13-0, won 23 games in a row, won a conference playoff and stomped the pancreas out of the No. 1 team in a national championship bowl game?

They did get in one last little insult. The press and coaches voted Florida State No. 2, although Miami already had proved, head-to-head, it was superior to FSU.

The implication was that the Miami that Bama ripped 34-13 in the Sugar Bowl Friday night just wasn't as good as everyone thought. Well, who's to say Alabama wouldn't have ripped FSU 34-13? Just a minor, but irksome, point.

I'm no coach, but I believe this club, on the night that it embarrassed the Hurricanes, was the best-prepared team I ever saw.

``I just direct traffic,'' Gene Stallings said Saturday. That's not entirely true, of course, but, to an extent, head coaches do direct traffic, and directing traffic includes hiring assistants. A mixture of old pros such as Mal Moore and Bill Oliver and newcomers like Mike Dubose give Stallings the best staff in America.

I also believe this is the finest defense I ever saw in college football. Oliver wouldn't go that far, and neither would Stallings, but, what the heck, I will.

``I've been associated with several good ones, but this is what you judge them by,'' Oliver said, meaning Alabama's stopping Miami in the big game. But he fondly mentioned Bama's 1979 defense. ``They rate up there together. Both could run, both played hard, both were unselfish.''

Oliver played on that great 1961 Bama defense that allowed 25 points. ``That one was a heck of a lot slower than this one,'' he said. ``But it was faster than everyone else in 1961.''

Stallings was an assistant at Alabama in 1961. ``I used to tell the players the 1961 team was an outstanding college defense,'' he offered Saturday. He noted that he was in pro ball, away from the college game, for years, but, ``It's hard for me to think there's a better defense than the one we had this year. There may be. Somewhere.''

Alabama's defense gave Miami more looks than Madonna's trashy book gets. Gino Torretta, the Heisman quarterback, would glance up and see John Copeland, the murderous defensive end, lined up inside, on the same side with Eric Curry, the other murderous defensive end. He'd glance up and see five defensive backs. Six defensive backs. Seven defensive backs.

Can there be a greater tribute to coaching than a team's winning a national title with a quarterback of such limited ability as Jay Barker? He's a great young man, but not a great QB. Perhaps one of his favorite Bible verses, Philippians 4:13, sheds light on his being a victorious quarterback. Look it up.

I arrived in New Orleans a week ago believing Alabama had a good chance to win. Then I thought it would win and said so in the paper. By game time I was telling another writer Alabama would win because it had a better team than Miami. I think it would beat Miami if they played tomorrow, and I think it would beat FSU.

You couldn't be around these guys a week without their confidence and laser-like focus rubbing off on you. Alabama's 145 players had an 11 p.m. o'clock curfew in New Orleans. None missed it; none was ever late for a squad meeting.

Will Alabama be favored to win the 1993 national championship? Probably not. But a year from now, folks may be saying this is the worst club they ever saw that went 13-0 and won 36 games in a row and won two playoffs and two national titles. It's going to be another monumental Bama year.

A word of thanks

In your hands is the result of an unprecedented endeavor for our newspaper--to publish in 15 days a book on the Alabama Crimson Tide's national championship.

It is a process--building a book--that normally takes three to six months. It took a whirlwind five days and nights by writers, typists, proofreaders, designers, photographers and technicians, and 10 more days by the printer to make it happen.

I hope that you draw as much pleasure from the national championship book as we at *The News* received as we saw it come together.

It is a sturdy book, without frills. That's how you have to build them when you do it in 15 days. We did not scrimp on the stories, though. This book has more great stories and pictures on Alabama's championship season and the Sugar Bowl game than you will find anywhere else.

It wasn't without troubles. One that I must confess immediately is my inability to match *News* photographers with individual pictures. There were just too many pictures coming from the lab too fast. The photos were by Bernard Troncale, Hal Yeager, Joe Songer, Steve Barnette, Charles Nesbitt and Mark Almond. Special thanks goes to Nesbitt, who showed up at 2 Sunday afternoon, Jan. 3, without anyone asking and announced that he was there for as long as he was needed. It was the next day when he went home.

Other indispensable players:

--Of course, the sports staffers authored virtually the entire book: Charles Hollis, Clyde Bolton, Kevin Scarbinsky and Jimmy Bryan. Sports editor Wayne Hester and editors Steve Martin, Charles Goldberg, Mike Kilgore and Doug Segrest made sure stories were where they had to be when they had to be there. And behind the scenes, clerks and interns did yeoman keyboarding work: David Knox, Sean Quigley, Randy Grider, John Hudson and Bryan Brasher.

--None of the season's game stories still were in our computer. They had to be retyped, thanks to Drew Bailey. Proofreading chores were handled by Kim Lathem, Andrea Kantargis, and Alicia Archibald, who dropped all of her advertising copy writing duties to give *The Championship Season* its final read. Mark Self and Charles Burttram handled promotion duties.

--Designer Lori Smith said *yes* to the project and worked two critical days and nights on six hours sleep.

--Color lab technicians Albert Pardue, Bill Barksdale, Charlie Freeman, Donald Eddy and Mike Freeman spun out the color pictures.

--Tommy Russell, Wes Trammell, Lamar Gregory, Deborah Battle, Keith Criswell, Travis Skinner and Doug Hayworth found a way to process the dozens of photos that you see in the book.

Had any one of those people--and probably several others I failed to remember--missed a single beat, this book would not have happened, at least not with the speed that it was produced.

To each I offer heartfelt thanks for a job well done.

Tom Bailey
Director of Special Projects
The Birmingham News